2131

LETTERS FROM LORD SYDENHAM
TO LORD JOHN RUSSELL

LETTERS

FROM

LORD SYDENHAM

GOVERNOR-GENERAL OF CANADA 1839-1841

TO LORD JOHN RUSSELL

EDITED BY

PAUL KNAPLUND

[1931]

AUGUSTUS M. KELLEY • PUBLISHERS

CLIFTON 1973

FIRST EDITION 1931

(London: George Allen & Unwin, Ltd,. *Museum Street,*
1931)

Reprinted 1973 by
AUGUSTUS M. KELLEY PUBLISHERS
Clifton New Jersey 07012

By Arrangement With GEORGE ALLEN & UNWIN LTD.

Library of Congress Cataloging in Publication Data

Sydenham, Charles Edward Poulett Thomson, Baron, 1799-
1841.
Letters from Lord Sydenham, Governor General of
Canada, 1839-1841, to Lord John Russell.

Reprint of the 1931 ed. published by G. Allen &
Unwin, London.
1. Canada--Politics and government--1791-1841.
2. Sydenham, Charles Edward Poulett Thomson, Baron,
1799-1841. I. Russell, John Russell, 1st Earl, 1792-
1878. II. Knaplund, Paul, 1885-1964, ed.
F1032.S97 1974   320.9'71'03   73-83159
ISBN 0-678-00737-3

PRINTED IN THE UNITED STATES OF AMERICA
by SENTRY PRESS, NEW YORK, N. Y. 10013

EDITOR'S NOTE

C. POULETT THOMSON, first baron Sydenham, brought the government of the Canadas out of the chaos which had existed with varying degrees of intensity for about a quarter of a century. Though his term of office lasted less than two years, it equals or perhaps exceeds in importance even that briefer span of time during which his predecessor, Lord Durham, administered the affairs of British North America. Durham did indeed with admirable prescience sketch a course to follow. Sydenham's views in regard to this course were less farseeing, but he made the ship seaworthy and steered it amid shoals and through breakers till a navigable channel was in sight.

During this critical period, the seals of the British colonial office were held by Lord John Russell. Before Sydenham, or Thomson as he then was, went out to Canada, he and Russell had been colleagues in the ministry of Lord Melbourne. And Sydenham, though a political upstart, was on intimate terms with Lord John Russell. Their views seem to have coincided on many political and economic questions and their friendship remained unbroken while Sydenham served as governor-general of Canada and Russell was his superior as head of the colonial office. In their private correspondence they were untrammelled by their official relationship. Sydenham criticized freely the suggestions offered by his chief and virtually compelled Russell to sanction the measures taken in Canada.

When writing privately, Sydenham could unburden his soul as regards Canadian men and affairs. That these opinions left their mark on those of Russell may be taken for granted, though we are not in a position to gauge their full significance. However, no doubt can exist as to the value of these letters in shedding light on the life and work of Sydenham. Some of the letters were printed in the Memoir published by his brother, G. Poulett Scrope, in 1843. But then Sydenham's outspoken criticisms of several Canadians had of course to be deleted, and in many other respects the texts of the letters and extracts found in the *Memoir of Lord Sydenham* have been altered.

The reasons which caused Scrope to exercise discretion in printing portions of his brother's correspondence no longer exist. Some of the suppressed passages are of considerable historical importance; and it is the purpose of this book to present an unabridged edition of nearly all the letters from Lord Sydenham to Lord John Russell, 1839–41, found among the Russell Papers at the Public Record Office. The copies are from photographs and although the handwriting is in some places rather difficult to decipher, the editor hopes that no mistakes have been made. Where a word has defied repeated efforts, this fact has been indicated in the text. The editor wishes to express his gratitude to the officials at the Public Record Office in London for permission to have the letters photographed, to the University of Wisconsin and the John Simon Guggenheim Memorial Foundation for the opportunity to examine the originals and for financial assistance in getting them photographed and to the Keeper of Public Records and the Staff at the public Archives of Canada for aid in studying the official correspondence between Lord Sydenham and Lord John Russell.

PAUL KNAPLUND

Madison, Wisconsin,
September 1931

CONTENTS

INTRODUCTION

A TRAGIC fate befell the men whom Britain sent to settle the affairs of Canada after the Rebellion of 1837. Four governors-general—Durham, Sydenham, Bagot, and Metcalfe—served only seven years, two of them virtually repudiated by the home government, the other two by Canada; each was overtaken by death in or shortly after the office had been relinquished; each aroused a storm of controversy and became the target of bitter personal attacks. Yet, they form a noble band. Seldom has Britain sent men to govern overseas of such high caliber, so greatly and variously endowed, so well-trained for their posts, so wholeheartedly devoted to their tasks as were these four. With the din of the controversies which then tore Canada subsiding and the smoke of battle lifting, we can see that none of them labored in vain. They all helped to build the framework of the present constitutional structure of Canada, lent a hand in training the people of British North America in the noble art of self-government, assisted in changing the course of British imperial policy and in revealing to Britain that freedom is the corner-stone of empire.

Viewed from one angle, the fate of Lord Sydenham was the least tragic of the four. He died feeling that his work was done—well done. Wills had been bent, obstacles overthrown, mountains scaled. He died triumphant, like Nelson in the cockpit of the *Victory*. But, on the other hand, he passed away at the moment when he felt himself fairly launched on a career that would lead to greater triumphs and bring richer rewards than any hitherto achieved. He was lonelier than the others. He had no friend or trusted counsellor at his side, no united host behind him. To him men and parties were but means to an end. With restless and ruthless energy he had striven for immediate success. It was gained. But his political system soon crumbled; the union of the Canadas in which he rejoiced lasted but a quarter of a century; the people to whom he gave his all—even life itself—have often reviled his memory; and History has been chary in its praise of C. Poulett Thomson, first baron Sydenham.

But the voice of the people is not always that of God, and the judgments of Clio are often reversed. Lord Sydenham deserves justice. Few men have faced problems so knotty as those which awaited C. Poulett Thomson when he landed at Quebec, October 19, 1839, as governor-general of British North America. True, the Canadian rebellions had been put down; Lord Durham had come, stayed about five months, acted decisively if not always wisely, left in high dudgeon, and produced a state paper on the situation in Canada which deservedly ranks high among the constitutional documents of the British Empire. The diseases of Canada had been diagnosed, not cured. Indeed the acts of Lord Durham while he was in Canada, his recall and his report, and the proposals for the settlement of Canadian affairs drawn up by the imperial government were at the moment additional sources of contention among the people of Canada. The old wounds were festering. Canada still presented the spectacle of "two nations warring in the bosom of a single state." M. Louis Papineau, the leader of the French in Lower Canada, and several of his lieutenants were in exile; other leaders had been killed or deported or languished in prison. The prize for which they had contended, an elective legislative council, was now definitely beyond reach. The constitution had been suspended and the province was governed by a small council appointed by the crown. The English element in the population, though greatly outnumbered, controlled the machinery of government. The French majority was defeated and branded as rebels. For the moment the French Canadians were cowed, not crushed. Canada was their home, and they formed a solid block controlling the gateway to the interior of British North America.

Lower and Upper Canada seemed in October, 1839, wider apart than ever. The old causes of dispute, arising from the geographical position of the lower province and the attitude of the French towards commerce, remained as before. But the hostility between French and English had increased. The Loyalists of Upper Canada urged the use of severe measures against the rebellious French.

Within the upper province passions ran high. Though William Lyon Mackenzie had been frustrated in his effort to break the power of the Family Compact and was now a fugitive, the discontent on the part of the majority of the inhabitants with the power and prestige enjoyed by a camarilla bound together by family and other ties and residing in and near Toronto had not been allayed. Indeed Mackenzie's appeal to arms had greatly intensified the bitterness of party strife, and the efforts of the Family Compact group to stigmatize all political opponents as traitors added fuel to the flame. Religious animosities did their share in keeping the two provinces apart and in causing dissentions within each of them. Protestant against Catholic, Wesleyan against Anglican kept the cauldron seething.

The civil service and the administration of justice had been faulty before the disturbances of 1837 and had grown worse since. In both fields a new system and stricter standards were sorely needed. Trade had suffered, immigration had been stopped, and the finances of Upper Canada were in a deplorable condition. Peace, order, and security, revival of trade and the filling up waste spaces with immigrants were remedies easy to suggest but hard to secure and apply. Still the government must provide and use them. Land, immigration, the relations with the various land companies, education, Clergy Reserves; local government, the seignorial system in Lower Canada, the state of provincial banking, the tariff and trade policy of Britain, each added a not inconsiderable moiety to the complex situation which awaited the new governor-general.

Nor were his duties confined to the Canadas alone. As governor-in-chief of all British North American provinces he must keep a watchful eye on the affairs of each. Nova Scotia was torn by political controversy and soon he was called upon to act as judge and arbiter in that province. Newfoundland needed attention and his advice was sought.

It has thus been shown that the internal affairs of the colonies supplied onerous burdens for Lord Sydenham, but they did not constitute the whole load. For some time past, Robert Baldwin and other reformers in Upper Canada had clamored for responsible government, a change which would alter profoundly the system of government within the colony and revolutionize its relations with the mother country. Lord Durham had advised the adoption of this reform, though neither he nor its advocates in Canada fully realized what it implied. Durham's support of responsible government naturally strengthened the Canadian demand for it. The reform party believed that here was a cure for the ailments of Canada. But nearly all British statesmen and politicians agreed in considering control of the executive by the legislative branch of the government a system totally unsuited for a colony. Consequently Thomson was instructed to govern the Canadians in accordance with their own wishes without conceding the reform which the most aggressive and politically minded in the population so ardently desired. He was expected to steer safely past Scylla and Charybdis.

Due in part to imperial and in part to local causes, the relations between British North America and the United States at this time presented difficulties of no mean proportions. Anti-British feeling ran high south of the international boundary, and in the British colonies the United Empire Loyalists and others nursed memories both of old wrongs and of injuries suffered in the war of 1812. Reasons for quarrels were not wanting. New Brunswick and the state of Maine had for some years been practically at war over the possession of a considerable tract of land along their border. Participants in the Rebellion of 1837 had found refuge in the United States and with the aid of sympathizers and adventurers they had established hunters' lodges and other means for keeping adjacent portions of Canada in a state of apprehension. The destruction of the *Caroline* in American waters during the rebellion and the aftermath of this exploit, the McLeod affair, created complications that easily might become serious. The existence of slavery in the United States and its absence from British dominions also in various ways helped to supply topics for disputes.

Nor was the United States the only foreign power whose relations with Britain affected the situation in the Canadas. It is a far cry from the banks of the St. Lawrence to those of the Nile, yet Sydenham watched the course of events on the latter with some anxiety. Although Papineau had failed to secure aid from the government of Louis Philippe, if the strained Anglo-French relations of 1840 should lead to war in Egypt and in Syria, French propaganda, if nothing else, might create serious embarrassments for the British authorities in Canada.

The problems, domestic, imperial, and foreign, that existed and threatened to arise in connection with British North America in 1839 were of a magnitude to daunt the bravest heart and to strain the resourcefulness of the most agile mind. The seriousness of them all were not known or apprehended in their entirety when C. Poulett Thomson in August of that year accepted the proffered governor-generalship of Canada. Still he did not rush in blindly. He had been a member of the Melbourne government when the clouds gathered and the storm burst in Canada, when Lord Durham went out to Canada and returned, when Lord Glenelg was driven from the colonial office on account of the Canadian troubles, and when Lord John Russell wrestled with his plans for a Canadian settlement. Moreover, for eight years Thomson had served as vice-president and president of the board of trade, the department which, next to the colonial office, was most intimately connected with all problems of colonial government.

This familiarity with the colonies in general and the Canadian affairs in particular, his reputation as an indefatigable worker, a skilful administrator, and a successful political strategist, and his friendship with the new colonial secretary, Lord John Russell, will explain why Thomson was offered the governor-generalship of Canada. It may not be so easy to understand why he accepted it. Thomson's health was delicate. He had access to and thoroughly enjoyed the cultured and polished society of London and other European capitals. Both physically and otherwise he was not adapted to the life on the frontiers. And indeed his sojourn in Canada proved to be for him a period of loneliness and torture. Some of this he could not have foreseen, but much of it he doubtless anticipated. Why then did he go?

In the first place, it may be well to keep in mind that despite Grèville's unflattering description of C. Poulett Thomson as "the greatest coxcomb I ever saw and the vainest dog" he was a man endowed with an iron will and with other masculine qualities required of leaders. Frontiersmen, as were those of Canada that submitted to Thomson's leadership, are not easily duped nor readily frightened. They saw in him a man qualified to lead, a guide whom they could trust. Not all among the leaders of opinion in Britain recognized Thomson as one who possessed these qualities. Greville did not, nor did Lord Melbourne, but Lord John Russell did. And Thomson himself had no doubts. Supreme self-confidence he possessed in a superlative degree. He knew that he could succeed where others had failed. Canada, the graveyard of reputations, would, he believed, give him a name.

In the second place, Thomson was ambitious; he felt

himself destined to do great things. Prolonged association at home with the moribund and discredited Melbourne ministry would further neither his fame not his political fortune. Something might be achieved in Canada. It will be seen from the letters that Thomson's heart was set on a peerage. This may, indeed, simply be an illustration of the vanity of which Greville speaks; but on the other hand, keeping Thomson's ambition in mind, it is well to remember that he was not an effective speaker. Ability to shine both on the hustings and in the House of Commons was required in order that a politician who did not belong to one of the great families could rise to pre-eminence. A peerage had not yet become a bar to the greatest offices in the government, and the lords though proud of descent recognized talent. Therefore, the peerage for which Thomson was so anxious would be a reward for service and a most useful asset in later life.

Thirdly, Thomson knew the views of the cabinet and he felt sure of the support of its strongest member, Lord John Russell. The real leader of the government was Thomson's closest friend. He did not apprehend a treatment such as had been meted out to Lord Durham. Many of the risks to himself personally connected with the governor-generalship of Canada were absent in Thomson's case. While to him the prospects of success threw open alluring vistas.

When less than two years after C. Poulett Thomson had first viewed the Heights of Abraham, Lord Sydenham lay dying at Kingston, a vast change had come over the land. He had been ruthless. He had cut and slashed, amputated and mended; the flesh was raw in places and the sutures hurt, but the patient was recovering. The shouts and kicks were those of a convalescent who refused to be confined. Though bandages had to be changed and new tonics administered, Sydenham had not bungled. In government no cure is permanent, no nostrum infallible.

Lord Sydenham rendered great services to British North America and to the British Empire. True, his system of cutting across party lines in forming a ministry and with himself, the governor-general, acting as prime minister, Gerrymanderer, and chief whip, was doomed to be short lived. But no other could have brought the results which he achieved in such an incredibly short time, and many of his reforms had to be secured quickly. By recognizing, as it did, the necessity for the ministry of keeping the support of a majority in the assembly, the Sydenham system bridged the gap between the old order of representation without power and the new whereby the government is the executive agent of the political party in control of the elected branch of the legislature. Similarly, the union of the two Canadas for which he worked so hard and from which he expected so much had to be broken up; but this union saved the situation in the early forties and it served a useful purpose as a prelude for the Confederation of 1867, when changed conditions and new problems had made a new political organization feasible. In politics and in administration, Lord Sydenham brought about reforms and changes, many of which have proved both salutary and lasting. Particularly in the fields of local government, education, and the judiciary, his work left indelible impressions. No other period of equal length in the history of Canada has been so potent in influencing the future development of the country in politics, law, and administration as was the term of Lord Sydenham's governor-generalship, October 19, 1839, till September 19, 1841.

In forming an estimate of the reasons for the success of Sydenham, credit must be given to Lord John Russell and allowance must be made for the fact that practically all Canadians—French, United Empire Loyalists, and recent comers—were monarchists with whom the royal will counted for much when proclaimed and represented as it was by Sydenham. Nevertheless all students of the period will be impressed by the importance of the personal factor. Sydenham did it. Let us admit that he was often hasty in his judgments and not overly scrupulous in his choice of means, still even a superficial survey of his work will reveal that the obstacles were many, the material to be mastered great, and the results remarkable. And all this was done while Sydenham fought physical pain. The strength of will, the firmness of purpose, the clarity of mind, the fertility of resource in this semi-invalid astound the observer. Sydenham was the business man in politics. His work in Canada forms in a measure a counterpart to that accomplished by Peel and his disciples in the government and administration of Britain, work achieved as much behind the scenes by injecting a new spirit in the administration as by adding new measures to the statute book. Behind and permeating the work both in Canada and in Britain one finds a new spirit which is not of the eighteenth century and but slightly related to political philosophy. The bewigged pomposities of the eighteenth century left an Augean stable to their descendants. Jeremy Bentham and his friends doubtless did something towards arousing their countrymen to emulate Hercules; but it may be suggested that the new spirit in business and in industry, created by changing economic conditions, was an even more potent force. Efficiency counted, and the old order of things both at home and in the colonies blocked progress. Sydenham represented the aggressive business ideals of his age. The go-getting spirit which he ridiculed in the Yankees he brought to bear upon the affairs of British North America. The business firm of his father and brother in whose service he had spent his youth seems to have been suspected at times of sharp dealings, and one has reasons to think that as governor-general of Canada, Sydenham was not particularly squeamish in his choice of means. He meant to succeed. With tireless energy he applied the business man's standards, his passion for system and order, to his task as governor-in-chief of British North America. They wrought wonders in Canada and rendered no mean service to the British Empire. And for Thomson himself, the path he entered in Canada led to glory and the grave.

LETTERS FROM LORD SYDENHAM

CHAPTER I

The government's Canada Bill. Criticism by Peel. Parliamentary strategy. Thomson's advice. Guarantee of Canadian loan. Views of Lord Howick. Clergy Reserves. Thomson's salary as governor-general of Canada. Instructions in regard to guaranteed loan.

LORD JOHN RUSSELL had for several years taken a keen interest in the affairs of Canada[1] and it was largely due to him that the incompetent Lord Glenelg was forced to resign the colonial secretaryship in February, 1839.[2] In June of the same year, Russell first introduced a series of resolutions dealing with Canadian questions and then a bill affirming the principle of a union of Lower and Upper Canada. On June 27th, Sir Robert Peel inquired whether the government was prepared to legislate in the present session on the union of the Canadas. He did not object to the principle of a legislative union, but he doubted the wisdom and the propriety on the part of Parliament to decide on the principle of a union without proceeding to actual legislation. If the government intended to limit its action to the measure now before the house and persisted in pressing it to a second reading, he would move the previous question.[3]

28 *June* 1839

PRIVATE

MY DEAR LORD JOHN

    Surely it would be better *not* to press the Canada Bill to a 2d reading after what was said by Peel last night, and the expression of opinion by some of our friends.

Peel declared himself favorable to the principle of the Union and that in quite as strong terms as we can expect. A debate and above all a division upon the previous question which he wd. move, might do our schemes mischief in Canada, and could do no good.

Might you not therefore say that you were satisfied with finding that the principle of the union was acknowledged by the two sides of the House, as no one had offered to oppose it, and that acquiescence having been obtained, you intended to proceed in Canada upon that understanding by employing the recess in getting the concurrence of parties there to the details of the plan, so as to be in a state to submit the measure as far as possible complete early next session to Parlt?

My opinion is that if you send out a proper person to Canada with your Bill, he may easily reconcile differences of opinion there upon the details, get a pretty general assent to some such plan as we have proposed, and send you back our amended Bill which you may pass next year. But to do that, it is far better that he should not be hampered by all sorts of conflicting opinions delivered in Parlt. upon those details, which would certainly be the consequences of a discussion *now* upon the Bill.[4]

Many people here have spoken to me in this sense.

Yours very truly

C. POULETT THOMSON

Canada continued to occupy the attention of the government during the summer of 1839. Among the Canadian questions discussed was that of guaranteeing a loan which might ease the difficult financial situation in Upper Canada and be used as a lever by the home government.

WHITEHALL 20 *Augt.* 1839

PRIVATE

MY DEAR LORD JOHN

    I put down on paper what I considered to be the decision of the Cabt. on Saturday on the guarantee of a Loan to the Canadas to be raised by them under certain circumstances. Normanby[5] wd. shew it you.[6]

    Howick[7] wanted quite a new condition to the settlement of Canadian matter, viz., that the question of Clergy Reserves was to be settled by the Upper Canadian Legislature as a sine qua non to the promise of a Loan on the settlement of the Union. Stephen[8] who knows this question thoroughly will explain it to you as he has done to Normanby since his return from you the absurdity of this suggestion. Even *Head's* assembly[9] could never agree with the Council upon the terms of distribution, and there is not the smallest chance of the two bodies being ever brought to concur upon it. But it will be done easily enough in the United Legislature, where of course care will be taken to have the two branches in harmony, and not split as at present. Of course it might be *tried*, and most likely the only important part, namely the utilizing the lands could be obtained, but not the distribution— and to postpone our Union till that question was carried in Upper Canada alone, would be deferring the Union not to 1842, but to the Greek Kalends.

    I should like you to see Stephen upon this point.

Ever yours truly

C. POULETT THOMSON

[P.S.] I wish you wd. send this to Ld. Melbourne, as I could not see him after I had consulted Stephen.

The governor-generalship of Canada was offered to Lord Clarendon, Lord Dunfermline, and perhaps others.[10] On August 5, 1839, the *Morning Chronicle* reported rumor that C. Poulett Thomson, the president of the board of trade, would be appointed to the post. Lord John Russell in a letter to Lord Melbourne of August 16th, suggested this change[11] and a week later Thomson had agreed to accept the post.[12] However, a misunderstanding arose over the question of his salary.

WHITEHALL 31 *August* 1839

MY DEAR NORMANBY

I am sorry to make objections upon such a subject but I cannot in justice to myself or to the appointment, consent to the important alterations you now propose especially after having taken every precaution in my power that there should be no mistake or misunderstanding whatever.

You informed me after the sitting of the Cabinet that it had been decided to add 1000£ to the sum proposed by you, making 7000£ a year salary; that this was to be paid from home and that any houses & incidental expences (of which I can form no estimate) such as going to Toronto etc., were to be defrayed in the Province. In order to prevent the possibility of any misunderstanding I wrote to you on Saturday the 24th what was my understanding of the proposal made to me & my acceptance of it. I read this to you & understood you to agree to it. I had also read it to Palmerston. This I did in order that the matter might be clearly & definitely fixed before I gave up my office or vacated my seat, and it being so, on the Tuesday following I had my writ moved.

I cannot consent *now* to have these conditions changed in the manner proposed in the letter to the Treasury. I have no notion whatever of the nature of expence to be incurred in removals during the winter from Lower to Upper Canada & will not undertake to bear them, tho' they shall be as economically managed as possible by me for the province. But above all I object to a change *now* in what I considered quite settled & upon which I have acted.

I return you my note of the 24th the words are "and the expence of removal."

I am sure that nothing can be further from your wish than to act unjustly & I certainly know it cannot be mine to adhere pertinaciously to any understanding expecially on such a subject, but I really cannot do otherwise than claim my right.

Believe me
Yours very sincerely
C. POULETT THOMSON

Sept. 1st 1839

MY DEAR THOMSON

I am sorry to find that there has been a mis-understanding on the subject of your Salary and expences in Canada, & I regret it the more as I am here without colleagues or advice & it appears there is no time to lose. I can have no difficulty in stating my recollection of what was agreed to at the Cabinet—a Salary of £6000 a year was proposed, with the payment of incidental expences & it was altered to £6000 with an additional £1000 a year to pay for journeys and removals.

It appears however that you have understood the

arrangement to be £7000 a year Salary & the payment of "the expence of removal."

Properly speaking, we ought to have another Cabinet upon this & you ought to be free to accept or refuse ultimate proposal. But it is too late now to assemble the Cabinet, or to give you this option.

Seeing therefore that your acceptance has been founded on a belief that you were to have a Salary of £7000 a year & your expences of removal paid, I am ready to take upon myself to recommend to the Treasury the Salary you have expected, & such additional sums for expence of removal to Upper Canada as may appear reasonable.

Of course I can give you no further assurance but I will speak to Lord Melbourne today or tomorrow and trust I shall obtain his acquiescence.

I remain My dear Thomson

Yours very faithfully

J. RUSSELL[13]

P.S. In explanation of one sentence of the above, I should say that I understand the general rule of the Colonial office to be, that any extraordinary expences of a Governor are submitted to the Secretary of State, and if thought reasonable by him, recommended by him to the Treasury for payment.

I propose in this respect therefore to follow the usual course.

WALTON 1st Sept. 1839

CONFIDENTIAL

MY DEAR LORD JOHN

Your letter is quite satisfactory, if as I doubt not the instructions to the Treasury are given in conformity with it. What you propose is, (if as I presume is meant the providing me with houses be intended) in exact accordance with what I understood from Normanby and put down in a letter which I read to him on the 24th Augst. & to which he agreed. This I inclose, requesting you will return it.

The Salary was a matter of very little comparative moment to me. I was informed that the Cabinet had fixed it at 7,000£ and altho' many of the members of it told me that they thought it too low, I offered not the slightest observation on it. It is easy for me in respect to living, entertaining etc. to cut my coat according to my cloth, and if I chuse to live more expensively than the Govt. think desirable, quite fair that I should live at my own cost.

But it is of essential importance to me, and to any man in his senses, not to undertake to defray expenses of which he can form no possible calculation, and nothing would have induced me to accept of any defined sum, be it 500 or be it 5000£, to compound for charges of which I know & can know nothing & which may or may not arise. It may be necessary for me to visit Toronto once or more often. It may not. It may be necessary for me to visit the other Provinces—it may not. Is there a house or a lodging at Toronto? will it be necessary for me to transport my baggage and establishment there? I cannot know. What will be the cost of these arrangements? It may be 50£, it may be a large sum. To attempt to compound for unknown charges would be ridiculous— I might receive too much which would be unfair—or I might be exposed to heavy charges unless I was cramped in my movements, which wd. not be desired. There is no precedent of any sort to guide me. No one before Durham held the office I do, and he only paid a flying visit of a day to the Upper Province.

It was on these grounds that whilst I offered not the slightest objection to the Salary proposed to me, as I understood it, by Normanby, I told him, and recorded it afterwards by letter in order to avoid all possibility of misunderstanding as Palmerston knows, that I could not and would not undertake to defray charges of which I knew nothing. My endeavours will be to incur as far as possible—none, if I can help it—but if they are necessary, they must be paid by the Public.

As a man of business I thought this the fairest way, because I know that it is always better to settle such things clearly beforehand, and understanding fully that this was done, I was not a little surprised and peeved at finding a Dft. letter to the Treasury sent to me, at variance with all the stipulations mutually agreed to.

There is an end however I hope now to this painful business—I do not think that if Saturday had been the *2d September*, it ever would have arisen.

I shall find you, I suppose, tomorrow.

Ever my dear Lord John
Yours very sincerely
C. Poulett Thomson

Downing Street *Sept.* 2 1839

[*Copy*]

Dear Thomson

There is one point of considerable importance, of which you will not find any mention in your Instructions. This letter will however convey to you a sufficient authority

upon which to act, so far as the present Cabinet are concerned. It was agreed at a meeting of the Cabinet, that
the Governor General should be authorized to promise
that Her Majesty's Government will submit to Parliament
a proposal to guarantee a Loan to Upper Canada or to
the United Province for the purpose of diminishing the
interest of the Debt, & of continuing the Public Works,
of a sum not exceeding one million & a half sterling.[14]

This loan is to be secured on the Revenues of the
Upper Province, or of the United Province.

This assistance is discretionary on the part of the
Governor General, & only to be used in order to obtain
the consent of the Provinces to what may be deemed by
him a final & satisfactory settlement.

I need not press upon you the reserve with which this
authority must be exercised in Canada, or the extreme
difficulty of obtaining the consent of the House of
Commons to such a proposal, unless the prospect of a
final & satisfactory settlement can be made clear, &
distinct to the people of the United Kingdom.

I remain, My dear Thomson

Yours very faithfully

(Signed) J. RUSSELL

CHAPTER II

THOMSON had several conferences with Lord Durham on Canadian affairs before he embarked at Portsmouth, September 13th, on the *Pique*, a sailing vessel, for Canada. On September 18th there appeared in the *Colonial Gazette* an article[15] which purported to give authoritative information regarding the views of the new governor-general of Canada. The paper was sent to America by a steamer and reached Canada before Thomson arrived.

Oct. 4 1839

MY DEAR THOMSON

I send you another letter from Ellice[16] written in a more friendly tone than those I have lately had from him. The publication in the Colonial Gazette was, I conclude, prompted by Durham, & in any view is most impolitic & unjustifiable. But I trust yr. Appointment of Sir Richard Jackson to be Lieut-Governor of Lower Canada in yr. absence, & yr. refusal to join in any movement for what is absurdly called responsible Government, will counteract the bad effects of this publication. The choice of the Chief Justice as the head of the Executive Government is of course out of the question.[17]

Sir G. Arthur[18] has sent me his answer to the Address respecting Responsible Govt. & I have approved of the tone of his answer, but recommended a cessation of the controversy *on his part.*

The Boundary Question will demand yr. attention.[19] Too much activity & too great forbearance are alike to be avoided. As far as things have gone, I think Sir John Harvey[20] has done very well indeed.

I remain

Yours faithfully

J. Russell

Quebec 22d Oct. 1839[21]

PRIVATE

My dear Lord John

Ellice's letter which you sent me is a thing of falsehood mixed up with just truth enough to deceive, and he sent it to you because he knew that I was not at hand to expose them, but as he owns to having sent his letter to the Chronicle, *because* he thought I was gone. But I shall not lose my time or your's in commenting on his conduct or exposing his untruths. He and his Brother[22] have fortunately failed in their endeavors, and I shall take no further notice of him. My reception has been particularly good, especially from the merchants, whose address was quite unusual, no preceding Governor having had one on his arrival. My Levee yesterday was more numerously attended than any one of Durham's, and the feeling here towards myself is certainly good.[23] This is advantageous so far as it is an answer to the London address,[24] and I believe owing to it—of course it is of little importance otherwise. One thing connected with it however, is—I find that the People here were really most anxious to have a Civil Governor sent out; when they found our Bill abandoned, & nothing done, they despaired of me, and were therefore prepared to receive me well. Colborne[25] too is not popular in Quebec with the British party on account of a local jealousy of Montreal which they supposed him to favor, and therefore they do not regret him.

Of course after only three days I can give no opinion of the state of things or of the chances of success. I have seen Colborne every day & had much conversation with him. His speech by the bye is the most striking contrast to his pen, for he is the greatest talker I ever met with. He thinks the Provinces are yet recoverable if the Govt. declares its intentions firmly, and will act *for* the people who want to be led. He considers the Union the best plan to adopt & that it is popular in the lower Province except with some of the *moderate* French party and the Priests, but these may be got over. In the Upper Province he anticipates great difficulty; the people have run mad upon "responsible Govt." and many of the so-called Govt. Party have gone over to that opinion. Arthur[26] too, he says, has, until within the last month, done all in his power to oppose the Union. Still, except at Toronto, he believes the majority favorable to it, and that it can and ought to be carried. He considers both Provinces as quite safe at present from either French Canadian or sympathising disturbances. I record these opinions of his because I think it right you should learn what they are as given to me *here*, especially as from what I have seen of him I am rather afraid they are not always very steady, and that his [illegible] is apt to be a good deal shaken by the last speaker. You can compare them with those he gives you when he arrives. I have of course shown him every mark of attention in my power.

I shall leave for Montreal tonight and I have arranged with the Chief Justice[27] to follow me directly—when there, I shall set to work with him and two or three members of the Special Council upon the Bill.[28] It will evidently want a good deal of alteration especially in the part relating to districts, but I think we can devise a substitute. However I must feel my way about the whole scheme. The time is the thing against me. I ought to have been here two months ago, for the communications with the Upper Province will be extremely difficult in another fortnight. But I will do my best.

Ever yours most truly

C. Poulett Thomson

The new governor-general moved rapidly. Leaving Quebec October 22nd, he arrived at Montreal the following day. Here he met with the special council entrusted with the government of Lower Canada, finished a large amount of business, left Montreal November 18th and reached Toronto November 22nd.[29]

Toronto 25 *Nov.* 1839

PRIVATE

My dear Lord John

I sent you from Montreal an official account of my proceedings with my Council respecting the Union,[30] and I am happy to find that the decision seems to give

great satisfaction in the Lower Province to nearly all
parties. Colborne seems to have been in the habit of
consulting everybody, but never urging any opinion of
his own—the result was that his council ran riot, and
did not know how to proceed. I have adopted à different
course, and have given my opinion pretty strongly, at
the same time that I expressed my willingness to hear
theirs. This course has shortened business very much for
there is a strong wish to be *led* by the Home Govt., and
has produced unanimity. So far then, as the Lower
Province is concerned, I look upon the matter of Union
as over with. This one, I am afraid will be a different
case. Yet the Union is ten times more required here than
there. If the People wd. submit to it, and the House of
Lords wd. give the powers necessary to make it effective
for good, a despotism wd. be by far the best thing for
Lower Canada for the next ten years. One might do ten
times the good that a House of Assembly will ever do,
and fit the People both for the higher and lower classes
of Self Government. But that cannot be. In this Province
however I firmly believe, that unless there be some great
changes, and I know of none that is practicable but the
Union, all is up. The state of things seems to me far worse
than I expected. The country is split into factions animated
with the most deadly hatred to each other. The people
have got into the habit of talking so much of separation
that they begin to believe in it. The constitutional party
are as bad or worse than the other in spite of their profes-
sions of loyalty. The Finances are more deranged than
we believed even in England. The deficit of 75,000£
a year; more than equal to the income. The Public
officers nearly one and all proved to be defaulters by an

investigation which is now going on. All Public works suspended—& emigration going on fast *from* the Province —Every man's property worth only half what it was. This is a pretty state of things to deal with, and I do not exaggerate it. The worst feature in my case is that I do not find here *one* man even in whom to confide or who can be of any assistance. In Lower Canada at least I had Stewart, a man of undoubted abilities, & strong man. The Govt. people are not worse than others, but they are as bad. I shall probably have to turn out the Atty. Genl. Haggerman[31] (sic) because he is opposed to the Union. But if I can I shall avoid doing so, as he has some followers. Still it will never do to leave *an open* question upon this point. The Solicitor Genl.[32] is fortunately a warm advocate for the measure. He and the Atty. Genl. battled it out last session for 5 hours apiece each night— think what a Govt! Arthur is disposed to render assistance, and as he is a man of powers, is I believe better trusted by my having left him in full possession of as many as possible, as well as by my having left him his house etc. But he is bewildered by the state of things, and I can now account for his dispatches. He finds a popular assembly quite another world from his council of convicts at Van Diemen's Land and has had no notion of dealing with them. Of my prospect of success therefore I can say nothing till next steamer. My endeavor will be to get the Legislature to agree to some resolutions upon the general principles of the union, as in Lower Canada, and to leave the details to the Imperial Parlt. Were I to enter into details with them I should be shipwrecked directly and with this effect, the Province too—for you may depend on one thing, that if another year goes over without a settlement this Province at least is lost. If I succeed in my plans, I shall then be able to send you a very good Bill, which you must carry, and which will certainly give satisfaction here, for any settlement will do that. The great complaint is that Parliament has *not* interfered—not as we have considered it likely to be, that it should interfere without consulting people here.[33]

Ever yours sincerely

C. POULETT THOMSON

[P.S.] Will you have the Chief Justice Robinson sent back as soon as you can.[34] It is abominable that a Chief Justice should be *nearly two years* absent from the Province. There is a case now standing over in consequence. The number of judges was increased two years ago on the ground that there were not enough, and yet the head of them takes his pleasure for two years. I understand that you have given him leave till the 1s March—but it is really too bad that he should stay away. People will not be contented to allow such things to go on, and with reason, besides which he will do you all the mischief he can in England. Pray have him sent now without delay.

TORONTO *Dec.* 1839

PRIVATE

MY DEAR LORD JOHN

The Legislative Council have voted a set of Resolutions which are all that I can wish. They approve of the principles on which the union is proposed, assent to the terms on which I offer it as between the two Provinces, and remit the details to the wisdom of the Govt. and Parlt. I hope you will think this is pretty well

managed, considering that last year, they wd. not agree
to the union itself even, upon any conditions. I got the
people up from the country, who really speak the feelings
of the masses and had the Toronto men who look only
to the value of their plots of land & houses, hollow.
Upon the division, Union or no Union, we had 18 to 4,
and upon conditions for the advantage of Toronto
14 to 8.[35] Six of the minority being Toronto men, and
the other two under their influence. Your confounded
Bishop[36] headed the opposition in all things, tho' I taxed
him with his promise not to engage in Politics. It was the
most numerous Council which ever assembled; nearly
double the number that ever voted before.

The House of Assembly have done nothing yet and will
give me infinite trouble, which is absurd, as more than
$\frac{3}{4}$th of them are decidedly for the Union. But they want
to attach all sorts of ridiculous conditions to it; not that
they believe they will be assented to, but that the Ultra
Tories who are opposed to Union think they may stop
the measures by getting them carried, and there are fools
enough amongst the rest to allow themselves to be per-
suaded into asking for them, in order to popularize themselves with their constituents, without considering that
they will lose the Union by it. If I had a man in the
Assembly to depend upon, I could overthrow this intrigue,
but my Law Officers betray me and I cannot afford to
part with them at this moment. However, if they per-
severe, now that I have got so strong an expression of
opinion from the Council, I shall dissolve the House at
once, and then I know that I can get a majority with
ease, and get rid of most of the Tories. Arthur is so completely bewildered with the state of things that he can

do me no good, tho' I believe he has the best intentions,
and the poor man has got a pleurisy into the bargain, so
that he has been in bed for the last week. I at last fished
out a man who really did me good service in the Council.
He is one of the best speakers I ever heard and would
produce no small effect in the House of Commons.
Oh, that I had him in the Assembly! By next mail I hope
to tell you the result of their deliberations, but I am not
sure for they are terribly slow. They have now debated
an amendment for three whole days from ten o'clock till
five or six, and when they get the Bill of last year which
I must give them tomorrow, they will probably discuss
all the clauses.

I have consulted many people here about the provisions
of this Bill with a view to a new one, and their opinions
agree altogether with those which I collected in the
Lower Province. I shall therefore have to send you the
heads of one differing very materially from our's, but
certainly very much improved. The Districts for Electoral
purposes will be altogether abandoned, and the present
divisions with a slight alteration adopted. The municipal
arrangement altogether remodelled, upon a smaller
scale, so as to avoid having five little Parliaments which
would be five great plagues; and the Legislative Council
remain as it is for life in the place of our eight years and
nonsensical *categories*. On this last point 1 have never
met with one man, Tory, Whig, or Radical who did not
think our scheme absurd.

The last Steamer, the Liverpool did not bring me a line
from you, tho' I suppose as you had not heard of my
arrival, you did not think it worth while to write. Still
I should be glad to get a word from you privately by next

Steamer, especially if you will say how you are getting on in Home Politics. I feel very desolate here occupied solely on Canada, tho' God knows that gives me work enough for the 24 hours each day.

I send you two other country papers which show the tone of the people. The Toronto press is violently abusive or the reverse and is no index of feeling.

My answer to the address of the Council has given great satisfaction, and I am told will help me in the Assembly. I hope so.

Ever your's most truly
C. Poulett Thomson

Toronto 18 Jan. 1840

PRIVATE

My dear Lord John

I have received by the New York Packet yours of the 30 Nov. & 3d Dec. Your new notions upon Clergy Reserves came a day after the fair. My siege of Malta was done. But why you should abandon your own first born (vide your letter of the Oct.) for such a miserable bantling as your second proposal, I cannot conceive. If as you say, it came from Lord Seaton,[37] it is only an additional proof that he was the worst civil Governor that ever ruled this Country, but I should not have expected from him such entire ignorance of the condition of Upper Canada. Why, in Upper Canada there are no tithes at all. You might as well try to get the breeches of the Glengarry & Stormont men, who wear none, as to get tithes from them. It is true that the Law gives them here, as in Lower Canada, but ever since the Country has been settled, except at Amherstburgh where there are a few

hundred old French Canadian Settlers, not an attempt
has been made to collect a tithe, and I should like to see
the man bold enough to propose it. But there are 40,000
Catholics and increasing numbers constantly arriving,
and indeed it would be the height of injustice to distribute
this property for religious instruction (difficult enough
God knows to get it at all for that purpose) without
providing for them like the rest of the Inhabitants. You
must treat this question on entirely different grounds in
Lower & in Upper Canada. In the Lower Province your
suggestion of a commutation of tithes shall be attended
to. It is certainly an anomalous state of things at present,
but no complaints are made—the clergy are paid—the
people are satisfied & *quieta non movere* in a Country where
so much is already in motion, and so much is to be done
is not a bad principle. But this scheme would have no
connection at all with the subject of Clergy Reserves in
that Province. There the Catholics would claim nothing,
because they would tremble for their tithes if they did,
and the matter will be most easily arranged by the
United Legislature whenever it meets. There are but
about 700,000 acres, and they may be sold for the
Protestant Church or for Education. In fact there is no
feeling upon the subject and never has been in Lower
Canada. But here the matter is quite different. The Clergy
Reserves have been, and are, the one great overwhelming
grievance—the root of all the troubles of the Province—
the cause of the Rebellion—the never failing watchword
at the hustings—the perpetual source of discord, strife
and hatred. Not a man of any party but has told me that
the greatest boon which could be conferred on the
Country would be that they could be swept into the

Atlantic and that nobody should get them, for after all there is little to divide; there will be nothing, after deducting the charges for the next ten or twelve years, but the difficulty lay in the Settlement. And where to this never failing source of excitement here, you had to add the consideration that by the Union, if you left the question in the Upper Province unsettled, you would throw the agitation of it into the Lower Province, where amongst all its ills, the greatest of all, religious dissension is hitherto unknown, the necessity for a settlement here becomes doubly great. Thank God, I believe I shall achieve it. My Bill, of which I sent you a Copy, has gone thro' the Assembly by a considerable majority 30 to 20;[38] and I feel confident that I can get it thro' the Council without the change of a word, for I can't trust it back again. There has been no alteration of importance except to substitute a division according to *numbers* amongst the different sects recognized by law, after giving the Churches of England & Scotland their half, instead of the division in proportion to contribution which I had proposed. I authorised the Sols General to state, in his opening speech, that they might have whichever they liked, and they preferred this mode. The Ultra Tories behaved in the basest way—they turned my Bill out *twice* in Committee by voting with the Radicals to appropriate the *fund for public works*—their names not appearing in Committee they did not care what they did. But my friends, altho' they were forced to vote for education or public works to redeem their pledges to their constituents, when they found what the Tories were at, declared "non tati auxelio" and rescinded every vote of this kind directly afterwards. So I got it to the third reading when these ragamuffins, having their names on the Journals, did not dare vote against Religious purposes & then I carried the Bill, as I have said, by 30 to 20. I now only wait for the Council, where I think I am sure.

If it is really carried it is the greatest work that ever has been done in this Country, & will be of more solid advantage to it than all the loans & all the troops you can make or send. It is worth ten Unions & was ten times more difficult.

You will laugh at me, but if it were possible to make you understand the state of feeling upon this subject, and the evils which this question has caused, which you cannot do, you would not. I confess too that I had little hopes of succeeding in the Assembly; for 15 years every Governor has only made the matter worse, and though I might have got the Council to agree to giving the funds to Education I never thought I could get the Assembly, which, for 13 years has voted for that and against religious purposes, to consent to such a plan. But I told you that I would work my popularity to some purpose and I have done it—ten members who had always before voted for Education or public works, voted for me this time, tho' they may lose their seats by it.[39]

23 *January*

The Council has voted my Bill by 14 to 5.[40] Today I have received the addresses of both Houses and the Bill goes home to you. The Bishop has excited his clergy to petition against it;[41] so you will have Phillpotts addressing the Crown.[42] You will remember that it is Dr. Strachan that we owe this matter being still open—15 years ago he might have settled it, if he would have given anything to the Church of Scotland; I have put a History of this question into a dispatch which you can lay before both Houses.[43] If the Lords reject the Bill, upon their heads be the consequences. I will not answer for the government of this Province, if the measure should come back. In case there is any blunder made by the Lawyers here, you must reenact the Bill in England, for *here* it cannot come again without the most disastrous results.

I send you home the Union Bill[44] and Pringle[45] to explain all matters connected with the representation, and the municipal Institutions. He knows them thoroughly. The Chief Justices' clauses will save you great trouble, and there will be little except the money clauses to prepare in England, but of course you must have the others thoroughly examined and amended.

You must take *a large Civil List*. Govt in this Country depends on your not being obliged to go to the Assembly for what you want. But upon this I presume that your experience of Lower Canada will make you feel strongly. Nothing short of the sums I have named and a margin to boot will do, especially if you give up again the duties under the 14 Geo. 3. The people here will be quite satisfied to have a large Civil List *taken* for them: they don't like voting it only. You may do this the more readily, because you will be called upon to help the Finances here by guaranteeing a loan, which will be indispensable to set up the United Province. As soon as I can get the Financial statements properly in order, I will send you a dispatch on this subject.

You will observe the clauses on the Gov. & Lieut. Governors. It will be absolutely necessary that for some months after the Union is proclaimed, the Lieut. Gov.

should remain in Upper Canada, but under the Commission he would have no power. This therefore must be provided for. But it is equally important that the Gov. should have the assistance afterwards of one or more Deputies to whom he may delegate functions. In a country like this, 1000 miles long, it is impossible for the Govt. to be conducted without such assistance. You may get very good men probably officers of some rank who would move about if required. You will have to pay your Governor General from England, because you must pay him well, if you mean to send Civilians when I have done my affairs. Military men have great advantages of fuel, forage, table money, rations, equal to probably 2 or 3000£ a year in this country and you must take this into your calculation in future. But certainly your Governor should be paid from England. I warn you of this, as I can have no interest in it.

You will observe that I do not propose to cut off Gaspé and Bonaventure which you did. The people there have petitioned universally not to be cut off from Canada, and they send two English members. It would be most unjust and unwise to transfer them to New Brunswick.

Believe me

My dear Lord John

Ever yours truly

C. POULETT THOMSON

TORONTO 13, *Feb.* 1840[46]

PRIVATE

MY DEAR LORD JOHN.

I have prorogued my Parliament and I send you my Speech.[47] I have carried my Union and my Clergy

Reserves; the Reform Bill and Irish Church of Canada, and my House of Commons gave me three cheers when the Speech was read which never took place before. I wonder when you will say as much of *your* Parliament! But seriously, the good feeling is not confined to the Members, wonderful as their's is, with the bad prospect at the opening; it is, I am happy to say, general through the Province, where the state of Public opinion is as different from what it was three months ago, as two things can possibly be. I don't think that Arthur can spoil matters for me now, tho' he is so weak that I am rather nervous at going. However, I mean to go through the whole of this Province in the Summer, which I believe to be one of the most important parts of a Governor's duty, and which will be still more necessary in order to know People before the Union, and therefore between that, and the Communications I am still here at Montreal; I hope that it will do.

I shall send you the necessary observations on the different Acts from below, and also a financial scheme for I cannot get them ready for the Mail.

Pray let me have your confirmation of my appointments by the return of the Packet. In these matters great importance is attached to no appearance of delay. I look upon it as an immense thing to have got Hagerman to take the seat on the bench. He had refused it three times from Colborne and Head, and would not have taken it now but I believe he thought his tenure under me was uncertain. I could have put no one else there well, either. Draper is a poor creature, but handy, speaks well, and is a fair man of business, & I thought it but fair to promote him from the Solicitorship. Baldwin is the best Lawyer in the Province and a man of the highest character. He is not in Parliament and I understand is not a good Speaker, but he is the man most esteemed and looked up to by the whole of the Reformers of Upper Canada, and carries that party with him altogether. He had at one time some rather extreme notions about responsible Govt., so before appointing him I thought it right to administer your Dispatch of the 14th Oct.[48] upon that subject to him, with every word of which he concurred. I consider his appointment as the greatest possible *coup.*[49] It is practically following up the policy which I have announced and acted upon, since I have been here, and to which I owe my Success—quietly to break up the Exclusive power of the Compact on the one hand, and repress the violent radicals on the other. The very violent of the first storm of course, especially as they see that I have silenced their great gun, Hagerman, and that without quarreling with him. The others can do no harm for I have got all their respectable leaders with me, and away from them. So now, if you will only send me back my Union and the Clergy Reserves, I will guarantee you Upper Canada.

But where *could* you get your notions on the Reserves from, which I find in the dispatch which I have acknowledged today?[50] Luckily, I sent you a history of this question,[51] or if the House of Lords is as ill informed as the Colonial Office, my Bill might have fared ill.

I have sent you a dispatch today about the distribution of the sum allowed to the Wesleyans.[52] Pray give me your assent at once to the arrangement I propose. I attach the *greatest* importance to this—and mind that Stephen[53] is not to be trusted upon this subject. He is wholly given to the London Conference, as is Arthur, who last year got

out a Mr. Alder to try and dethrone Egerton Ryerson
and only signally failed.[54] The Upper Canada Conference
is the most powerful body in the Province, and does the
greatest possible good, for which it has been very badly
treated. It is thoroughly Whig—with your Government;
whilst the other is bitterly opposed to you in England,
and the Leaders, for they have few followers, will do
everything against mine here, because I won't persecute
the Catholics. Arthur, to do him justice, was not aware
of the turn the Wesleyans took in England upon the
Education question, or he would not have patronized
them.[55]

Will you attend to the additional remarks I have sent
you on the Union Bill?[56] I am very much inclined to
Stuart's advice about the Civil List in these Colonies,
not to take one, but to keep the Crown Revenues and the
14, Geo. 3. It was a great mistake ever asking for a Civil
List in these Colonies, when you have a sufficient revenue
from Crown Property. Nobody thanks you for giving
them up, and everybody grumbles at what is paid in
return for it.[57] Besides, you cannot get on without some
funds beyond the control of Parliament—the People have
no discretion, and would refuse the most necessary
expense if asked for by vote, when they are in a bad
humour. It is not in these young Countries as in England,
where no party ever dream of stopping the Public Service
upon certain points, let the distrust of Ministers be ever
so great. However, it may be too late now.

I hope to hear shortly that you have made a good
opening. I only regret that my Settlement of the Union
could not have reached you in time for your Speech.[58]

Ever yours most truly
C. POULETT THOMSON

CHAPTER III

Returns to Lower Canada. Lamentable condition of the province. Hostility of French Canadians to everything English. The boundary dispute. Anti-union petition. Ignorance of English newspapers. Observations on home politics. Situation in Nova Scotia. Thomson's peerage. Agreement with Lord Melbourne. The launching of the Union Bill in the House of Commons. Complaints of changes in the Bill. Clergy Reserves. Aid for immigrants. Civil list clauses in Union Bill. Asks for legal adviser. Clergy Reserves and Lord Ripon. Municipal institutions for the Canadas. Thomson's title. Affairs of Nova Scotia. The boundary question. Work of Special Council of Lower Canada. Electoral districts of Upper Canada. Edward Ellice. Clergy Reserves. The boundary dispute. Views of the United States. The peerage.

THE Governor-General left Toronto February 18th and reached Montreal on the evening of the following day.[59] He immediately set to work to study and provide ways and means for improving the conditions in Lower Canada, but was a bit appalled by the task.

GOVT. HOUSE

MONTREAL 13th March 1840

PRIVATE

MY DEAR LORD JOHN

The Gt. Western brought me yesterday your letters of the 19th February. Your other letters, if there are any since the 3rd December, and many dispatches are still missing along with some twelve Liners which are over due. I am very much obliged to you for the kind manner in which you acknowledge what I have done, both in your letter and your public dispatches, and I feel it the more because it contrasts with that of another, from whom I should have expected *good faith* at least, if no praise. However, whilst *I am* here, neither he nor you shall have to complain of my neglecting my duty because my personal feelings may be wounded— so to business, of that hereafter.

You will have seen that I have achieved your "Wonders" on the Clergy Reserves. I hope that you may be right in your anticipations of Philpott's[60] want of power to do mischief, for I am sure that he has the will—tho' I believe he wd. not find a seconder if anyone of your opponents in the House of Lords could see the difference in the social state of Upper Canada now, from what it was three months ago, in some degree owing to the settlement of this question. John Toronto[61] is still busy getting signatures to his Petition, but I trust that it may be all over before they can arrive, for you will of course have laid the Bill on the table immediately, and only thirty days are given for an address. Upon this point, as well as upon the Union I am impatient for a decision, for I am afraid of Arthur in the Upper Province, now I have left it. Nothing can be better than it is now; but well intentioned as I believe him to be, he is the weakest and most *fussy* man with the narrowest mind I ever met —and fast relapsing, as I perceive, from his letters, under the influence of the party which ruled him before, altho' he professes and I believe really deprecates their power, I long to be able to work to get the whole thing under one strong government which I will work to some purpose, and principally thro' the Upper Canadians who bad as they are, present with the single exception of the Chief Justice, far better materials than these People.

I have now been back three weeks and have set to

work with them. It is a bad prospect and presents a
lamentable contrast to Upper Canada. There, great
excitement existed, but at least the people were quarrel-
ling for realities—for political opinions, and with a view
to ulterior measures. Here, there is no such thing as a
political opinion—no man looks to a practical measure of
improvement. Talk to anyone upon education, or public
works, or better laws, let him be English or French, you
might as well talk Greek to him. Not a man cares for a
single practical measure, the only end, one would suppose, of a better form of Govt. They have only one
feeling—the French hate the English and would cut all
their throats if they could—the English hate the French
and only desire to ride rough shod over them. The only
way therefore in which I can do any good is to do without
any of them and wait for the Union in order to get a
Govt. together, and this I shall do. I shall have an
excellent Judicature Bill remodelling the whole administration of justice (or injustice). I hope to get a good
system of education. I shall get elementary municipal
institutions thro' the Province to dovetail in with those
of the Union Bill—and I have a good Stipendiary magis-
tracy and Police force throughout. By the bye, the only
sensible thing which Lord Seaton did here was to
commence the organization of a rural Police, which I
have greatly extended and shall shortly make general.[62]

Your dispatches came in so late that there is no time
to reply to any of them by this mail but in ten days the
other Steamers' mail will be made up. I will attend
directly to your instructions about the Maine business.
Harvey[63] wished to withdraw even the troops from
Temisquata lately, but Jackson[64] by my directions

positively refused. It is clear to my mind that we must make an agreement (provisionally) with the Central Govt. of the U.S. which shall bind *them* to co-erce Maine —otherwise a conflict must ensue. I will use all my endeavors for this.

I have written you a confidential dispatch about the Anti-Union Petition[65] as well as the public one upon it, however I thought it right to record the facts in your office. But as I do not wish to irritate either Priests or even Rebels, it should not go to the table of the House of Commons on any account. I am not the least afraid of the effects of all this apparent opposition, especially since I have seen a good many of the French during the last week from different parts of the Province—they are now rather sorry for what they have been about, and had I been here or at Quebec, I am sure that I could have stopped all except Mr. Neilson's first Petition. Part of that is Quebec jealousy of Montreal or a place in Upper Canada being the seat of Govt. The choice of the Seat of Govt. must be left entirely to the Crown without giving the Parlt. any power to alter the Prerogative. I have left it so purposely, for no man can say where the first Parlt. ever ought to be held, and it is not unlikely that we must found a new capital. Kingston perhaps, for Bye Town is too cold and too far, tho' that wd. in other respects be the best place.[66]

How horribly ignorant your newspapers are of Canadian affairs. I am rejoiced that we have been two whole months without them. I see the Colonial Gazette making out that by the Clergy Reserves Bill I had turned all the Liberal party against me, upon the strength of an article in the Radical paper the Examiner,[67] the editor of which was brought on his knees to ask pardon the next week by the whole of the Reform members! The only decent paper in both Canadas is the Christian Guardian[68] which I hope they get at the Col. Off. I have ordered it to be sent.

I am delighted that the Tories have given you battle fairly and got such a drubbing—but I am alarmed about your financial state. I have had, to be sure, desperately hard work night and day for the last five months but I think that now I have got rather the pull upon Francis Baring,[69] especially as I have suffered less from illness than a fortnight of the House of Commons would have given me. Yet I can't help *seeing* the debates only with rather a sigh.

You will I think support the double fatigue of Colonies & Leadership—for God knows that it all hangs upon that.

Ever yours very sincerely
C. POULETT THOMSON

[P.S.] They have used me most scurvily at the Col. Off. about my letters. Pray let some arrangements be made by which I may be charged the Postage and they may come as usual in the Bag. I never can tell whether I shall be at this place, at Quebec, at Toronto or where, & the messenger from New York unless he can get my letters in the bag, cannot get them at all. Now, I suppose that half of them are gone to Toronto.[70] Sir C. Campbell is playing the dunce at Halifax.[71] The House of Assembly are quite wrong, but he is equally to blame. With the least degree of tact he might have managed them, and either prevented the blow up or made it appear that they were clearly bent on mischief. His time is up and I do intreat you to send a decent *Civil* Governor. He has held no communication with me or I wd. have advised him, but after all it is tact and usage which is necessary in dealing with popular assemblies, and if he has not got it as is clearly the case, no advice wd. do any good.

Having achieved the main objects for which he had been sent to Canada Thomson felt that his reward should not be delayed.

GOVT. HOUSE MONTREAL 26 *March* 1840

CONFIDENTIAL

MY DEAR LORD JOHN,

It is with the utmost reluctance that I address you upon any personal matter—you have enough to do without such calls—but I know that I can rely upon your friendship; and as except Ld. Duncannon,[72] you are the only person cognizant of my transactions with Lord Melbourne previously to my quitting England, you are the *only* one to whom I can with propriety apply at present.

Lord Melbourne has, as I conceive, departed from the most serious engagement towards me, one, which appeared to me beyond all question—a circumstance so unlike all that I know of him that I cannot believe that he has either referred to the terms of his engagement, or considered the effect which what he has done must have upon my feelings and my position. Here I have no friend to consult and none to advise with—I have however taken time to reflect upon the matter, and however my feelings may be wounded, I have determined that no personal considerations shall stand in the way of my discharge of my duty. I shall therefore await the result of my two measures in England, and content myself for the present by placing the matter in your hands.

Before I state my case however, I must, as you happen to stand in the situation of my Chief, guard myself against the supposition that I appeal to you in that character for any reward or acknowledgment for any thing I have done here. If I have deserved any, it is not my intention to claim it. I should be perfectly willing to wait your own estimation of any service I may have been able to render, and I can most truly say that the kind expressions you have employed in your letters, and the satisfaction I have myself derived from the success I have had the good fortune to obtain, have been more welcome to me than anything else could be. Upon this point there shall be no misunderstanding. The injury of which I complain, shall not be hereafter said to arise from an exaggerated opinion of my own merits, or from disappointment of a premature claim founded upon them. My case, is a breach of contract.

You know that I pressed Lord Melbourne, as a preliminary to my undertaking the govt. of Canada to give me a Peerage. A great deal of discussion took place upon the subject and various modifications were suggested on both sides, both verbally and in writing. At last, after an interview in which it was fully treated, Lord Melbourne had the following letter to Duncannon given to me.

"28 July [1839] I had some conversation with Thomson this morning upon the subject of Canada, and in order *to avoid both present and future misunderstanding* I thought it better to put down in writing what I conceive to be his own wishes and my own intentions. I am unwilling to confer the Peerage merely on account of his undertaking the duty, but if he should undertake it, and bring it to a successful issue, or conduct it so far as to bring it within view of a successful termination, I should consider a Peerage the *Instant result* & by no means too great a reward for so eminent a service. But I should be reluctant to bind myself to advise the Queen to this effect in case either the state of his health, the breaking up of the administration, or any other accidental chance should compel him to relinquish the task when he had only just commenced it & had made no progress in it. I wish you cd. explain this to him & settle when he is willing to embark upon this undertaking."

Two considerations presented themselves to me. First, what was meant by a successful issue—tho' this was not of much importance as the words were so qualified as to maintain the pledge even if I failed, thro' no misconduct of my own. However, I asked this question both of Ld. M. and in the presence of the whole Cabinet repeated it, and received for answer that obtaining the consent of the Provinces to the Union was full and complete success for I could not be responsible for what party might do in Westminster. The other point upon which I did not consider Ld. M.'s letter sufficiently explicit was the contingency of Ld. M. going out before I could fulfil the above condition, by which my Peerage might fall to the ground. Accordingly I applied upon that point and received the following reply[73]: "With reference to the letter which you gave me from Thomson yesterday I consider the case which he states to be comprised within the terms of my former letter, but if he has any doubt upon the subject, I have no objection to adopting the express terms which he has used and to undertake that if I should quit the government at the beginning of the next session, and that his conduct should (as I doubt not it will be) have been such as to establish that he had done all in his power for the fulfilment of the object of his mission, I wd. recommend him to the Queen for a Peerage" (31st July) [1839].

Upon these assurances I undertook the task—you know under what disadvantages, and with how little expectation of success on the part of either the Cabinet or the Public.

Having gained the assent of both Provinces to the Union, and that upon terms which terminate it as regards myself, for they are left to the uncontrolled discretion of the Govt. and Parliament, I of course claimed from Lord Melbourne the fulfilment of his part of the bargain.

To this I received the following reply—11th Feby. [1840]. "You may depend upon it that I will not quit office without doing my utmost to secure your Peerage, but *the time you must let me judge*. There are many circumstances of which where you are, you cannot be aware!!!" and I have received a message thro' a friend with whom I had *not* communicated, but he did, to this effect "that my head was turned by success, and that till the Union Bill was thro' Parlt., nothing was done."

I wish to add *no* remark to this simple statement of the case, for I do not believe that a single man could be found who would say that under the terms I have here repeated, Lord Melbourne had any, the slightest right, to withhold his performance of the agreement. The very words used by himself *"Instant result"* at once fix the time, and remove all discretion to which he now lays claim. It is just as if a man who has given a Bill at 6 months date, when it falls due, should say to his Creditor, "I am very sorry, but there are circumstances of which you cannot be aware which prevent my paying you." Would that be admitted as an excuse? or is it not still more unfair upon me, as I am thereby exposed to a number of contingencies, anyone of which might defeat the condition entered into with me?

I cannot believe, as I set out by saying, that Lord M. really reflected on the engagement into which he had entered. If I thought so, I should have some difficulty in following the course which I propose to myself. But I submit the case to you in order that you may both judge of it, and obtain from Ld. Melbourne that consideration which I *hope* has not been given to it. It is true indeed that situated as I am, the necessity of correspondence aggravates the injury which I conceive is done to me, and answers all the purpose of time against which I protest—but of course I am helpless unless I am prepared at once and under the uncertainty, to sacrifice my duty both to the country and yourself to my personal feeling, which I will not do, though I fairly own that under my present feelings my task here is rendered much more difficult, and I have little spirit to continue the exertions which I have hitherto endeavoured to make.

Once more I must beg your indulgence for intruding a personal matter upon you, but I have no option.

Ever your's most sincerely
C. POULETT THOMSON.

GOVT. HOUSE MONTREAL 5 *May* 1840

PRIVATE

MY DEAR LORD JOHN

I have only a few lines from you of the *2nd March* by some roundabout conveyance since I wrote—nothing since Pringle got home, tho' I have your official Dispatches of the 20 and am much obliged to you for your kind dispatch of approval by the Queen of what I have done.[74] The Gt. Western is not yet in, nor can we get her letters now, before my messenger starts, which he must do tonight, to take the dispatches for her return voyage. So I shall know nothing of the fate of my Bills. You launched the Union Bill admirably on the 23d.[75] Your statement of the provisions and of the reasons for them, was all I could desire, and has produced a very good effect here. Pringle however seems to have got you into two scrapes both of which I must beg of you to get out of without delay. He has cut down the Cy of Lincoln from four ridings each returning one member, to one county with only one.[76] This will never do—you must divide it into two ridings at least, as I proposed, with a member each; and why when you had an additional member to give Upper Canada he should step out of his way to commit such an act of injustice I cannot conceive. That additional member you may give if you like, either to Niagara or Cornwall, but I would rather not give it to either, but to another County, Durham. On the first point I feel so strongly that I have written to you officially. I can never show my head in the Upper Province after such an act of atrocity to Lincoln, where many of our best friends reside, and which they represent. The second scrape is, as he writes to me, that *he* prevailed on you, against your first directions, to produce with my dispatch upon the scheme, a list of representation, *not* as I sent it, but as it was afterwards altered!! In the first place this would make nonsense of the dispatch, 70 members recommended, & 78 places in the list; and next, it would be an absolute forgery. It is of course in your discretion to withold any passages, or the whole of any dispatch, you please, but to *alter* them is of course out of the question, and no wonder that you demurred! If he really prevailed on you to do this, pray let the correct list as I sent it, be substituted immediately. It is of great consequence to me in the Upper Province.

It is idle for me to speculate upon the fate of the Clergy Reserves, which must have been long ago decided. Ld. Melbourne's letter of the 25th March is very hopeless, but the later accounts I have from other's of the 30th say that *you* had good hopes. But if the Bishops have really bucked it, you will I hope have done one of two things—either settled the appropriation by a Bill yourself, or have proposed to remit the matter to the United Legislature, *free* from the clauses of 1791 referring their decision to either House of Parliament. To send it back here, rejected on account of its being too liberal, and still fettered by an address of either House would be the ruin of the Colony, and extinguishes all chance of the United Legislature doing any good or indeed of its being fit to do any. The first vote of the new Parlt., Assembly and Council, would be to devote the Revenue to Public works—open war with the Imperial Parliament—but besides this, you will have quite different members returned from Upper Canada under those circumstances. The elections will all go upon this question—the most

violent radicals who have now no chance, will all be
returned and I will certainly not answer for the consequences, when they are aided by the French Canadian
party. If this were to be, I pity my successor who would
then have to meet the United Parlt.

I have asked you in a dispatch to let me have authority
if necessary to draw 5 to 6000£ from Imperial funds for
the Emigrants.[77] Pray do, for I really have no idea what
I shall do with the numbers who are said to be coming,
in consequence of Sir John Colborne's folly in fixing his
ordinance to the 1st November, and thus rendering it
impossible to renew the Emigrant Tax. I have not a
sixpence in the Treasury, and no means of raising anything for any public purpose. It is impossible almost
to believe the mismanagement of Sir John Colborne in
all money matters. He threw away money right and left
upon the most absurd undertakings and entered into
engagements without end. I have had to legalize expendi-
tures of his, undertaken without any authority, out of
the Provincial Funds to the extent of 50,000£!! nearly
half the revenue of the Province, and he has left me
engagements to nearly as much. If the Revenue had not
luckily yielded 30,000£ more than was calculated, we
must have stopped payment. So I have litterally (sic)
no means of paying a pound either for Emigrants, Public
works, or Courts Martial, and of course under the powers
of the Act; none of increasing the revenue. Yet the
Revenue is nearly double the *ordinary* civil expenditure.
It is very provoking!

I don't much like your being beaten so often. I seem
to get an account of a fresh minority every packet—the
last, Stanley's Bill—but I hope they don't tell as much

with you. You will of course dissolve, if they become too "obstructive."

I am a good deal better—but not yet quite free from gout, & the weather is abominable, and much against convalescence.

Ever My dear Lord John

Yours most truly

C. POULETT THOMSON

P.S. I hope you gave Parliament *all* my dispatches on the Clergy Reserves. I kept up a strong fire for the purpose. You had better give Mr. Packington (sic) one I send today about the U.S. University with the inclosures. The Bishop is a regular swindler as will appear pretty evident.[78] I believe that I ought to have taken him into the Court of Chancery where he would have been obliged to account for every farthing. I really could not believe that such conduct was possible, but it shows how things were managed by the compact.

GOVT. HOUSE, MONTREAL 6 *May* 1840

PRIVATE

MY DEAR LORD JOHN

The Gt. Western Mail arrived today and brought me your's of the 2nd and 14th April, the dispatches, and the Bill. I have a chance of yet making New York before she sails, and I dispatch a messenger tonight therefore, tho' what I can say must be both short and hurried.

First, let me thank you for your letters. I feel your kind expressions most sensibly, and am very grateful for them. Whatever *you* wish, or think can assist *you* in your Govt., I will do in spite of Lords or Bishops at home, or disagree-

ments here, which now & then [gets] one out of humor
—as long at least, as they leave me a chance of doing
good.

I think your Bill will do, except a few inaccuracies
which I have pointed out in a dispatch,[79] and your Civil
List clauses & Crown Revenues. But these last are the
D——l and all, and *must* be changed. Who on earth framed
them? I wish I had sent them myself. The schedule to
which you propose to tie me down, as I understand it,
would in the first place knock over my Judicature Bill
here, the best work ever undertaken in the Province,
and next, provide nothing for Upper Canada Justice
which of course was included in my estimate. The
concession of the Crown Revenues *without* any of the
charges to which the faith of the Crown is pledged,
without the expences of carrying the Bill into operation,
without providing for the necessary retirement of many
Public Officers consequent upon the Union would
compel me to break faith for the Crown, prevent me
from working out the Bill as I ought, and force me to
keep the whole of the present vicious system of administration in both Provinces standing, which it is my great
object to remodel. It would compel me to come as a first
step to the Assembly for money for the most unpopular
of all purposes, paying the debts of the Crown, and
pensioning useless public servants. The provisions must
have been framed in the most careless way, for it is
actually proposed to allow of only 5,000£ pensions,
making no provisions for the fact, when in my account
sent to you, the Pensions *exclusive* of the Judges, are at
this moment 55,000£!!!

Pray have a proviso added to the 53d Clause providing

for these charges; this C. J. Stuart[80] says is the proper way, and I agree with him,

I don't much admire your change about the Municipal Govt., but I suppose you were afraid of the detail in the House of Lords, & so I must do it myself. But this renders it absolutely necessary that you should send me out a Lawyer. I cannot positively do without assistance, and you know me well enough to be sure that I should not ask it, if I did not feel it indispensable. So you must pay one from home to come out to me without delay. I write to Le Marchant to find one or help to do so. At this season of the year, such a man may be got to come for the job, easily enough; one who has had to do with corporations &c would be the best, but secure one who can understand, and give the time to the consideration of Acts, Proclamations, and Letters Patent, I *must* have, Stewart bests me at law, and tho' I work both day and night, I cannot attend closely enough to the details of such things.

I fear—from what you say that the Clergy Reserve Bill is lost so far as receiving the assent of the Crown goes, but that you will settle the question by an act re-producing its provisions. If you do that all *may* be right—but again I say the question *cannot* come back here with any safety to the Province. There will be disturbance enough in Upper Canada even if it is re-enacted word for word. After all, the Chancellor only thinks the infringement of the act of 1827 illegal, which I stated to you was so—tho' it certainly never was for one instant intended by that act to destroy the powers conferred on the Provincial Legislature by that of 1791. I hope by the bye, that you have saved me from imputation, by showing that the doubt with regard to the act of 1827 had not escaped me, and that I only did that which Lord Ripon, who now I see attacks me,[81] did upon the Trade act; offer to get a Provincial act which was against an Imperial Statute legalized. You will find a dispatch of his in which he invites the Canada Assembly to pass an act on this subject which they could not legally pass, under a promise that if they would, he would introduce a Bill legalising what they did: and if I am not very much mistaken he did the same thing when he directed a Bill to be prepared in U.C. vesting all the Revenues and proceeds (those in England included) in the Crown.

However I will not yet give up the hope of your "providing Bill" going thro', and the assent being given to mine, for God knows what the Lords would do with a fresh one. If it came to give any exclusive privileges to the Church of England, you will have a rebellion as sure as that the sun will rise tomorrow. So do not assent to anything of that kind.

Ever my dear Lord John
Your's most truly
C. POULETT THOMSON

GOVT. HOUSE MONTREAL 18 May 1840

PRIVATE

MY LORD

The Alteration which has been made in the Union Bill with regard to the establishment of municipal Institutions for the districts of Upper and Lower Canada, by which the Governor General is invested with the duty of establishing these Corporations by Letters Patent, instead of the whole detail being enacted in the Bill as originally prepared by me, render it necessary that I should no longer delay to apply to your Lordship for assistance to enable me to carry into execution the objects contemplated by Parlt. and H.M.'s Govt. Independently of this alteration, I should probably have felt it my duty to do this, but under the consideration of the prospect which I now see before me, namely that only Six months are allowed for carrying the Union into operation, and that I am also to be charged with this additional work, I am compelled at once to solicit the aid which I require, and to state frankly that without it, I cannot undertake the task which is likely to be assigned to me.

The assistance which I require is that of an able and experienced Legal Adviser.[82] I forebore, as you are aware, when I stated the amount of the establishment I required on quitting England, from engaging any Gentleman to accompany me in that capacity, and I have hitherto been able to do without such assistance, but I am not competent to perform the duties which the carrying into effect the Union Bill will impose upon me, without the aid of a Confidential Person in that capacity. There is no assistance to be obtained here of the character which I require, except such as I can receive from the Chief Justice of the Province of Lower Canada, which alone is not enough. My duties will necessarily call me to the Upper Province in the month of July and probably detain me there till the autumn—and in my absence more especially, but during my presence also under the circumstances, it is indispensable that I should have some person of legal attainments in whom I can confide, for preparing the details of measures which shall carry out my views.

I have therefore, to request that Your Lordship will be pleased to send me out without delay some Gentleman in this situation. As the duties for which I shall require his assistance cannot employ him more than four or five months, I should hope that there will be little difficulty in procuring the services of some one well fitted to render the assistance I require. Could you select a person conversant with the details of the municipal system in England, and practically acquainted with the details of the English or above all of the Irish County system, it would be most desirable. Some Barrister of character and abilities however I must have, and I repeat that without such aid, I should feel myself wholly unable to perform the task expected of me.

No time must be lost in obtaining such assistance either. It is my intention to proceed to the Upper Province in July, and it is necessary therefore that the gentleman whom you may select should be here before that time.

I have the honor to be

My Lord

Your faithful Serv.

C. POULETT THOMSON

GOVT. HOUSE MONTREAL 23d *May* 1840.
CONFIDENTIAL

MY DEAR LORD JOHN

Thanks for your letter of the 29*th* ulmo. As you say that the Queen's pleasure has been taken about my Peerage, I am quite satisfied: tho' I cannot altogether agree with you about Lord Melbourne.[83] But it is not my habit to keep up grievances. I wrote to him some time ago in reply to a letter from him asking about my title, that if he did not like to give me one connected with this country which would really have been serviceable, and any one obstructed (tho' no one had a right to do so) my taking "Waverly" I really begged that he or you would be good enough to make one—I feel utterly indifferent on the subject. I hope this may have been done, but lest it should not, I write to my Brother to settle this weighty matter with you, and then I rely on you to let the thing be gazetted at once, and without any further delay which I do not consider fair upon me.

I am extremely obliged to you for your promise to C. J. Stuart[84]—he is overjoyed—and it will produce an excellent effect in the Colonies by showing the People that talent and services in a Colonist may be really rewarded by the Crown.

I am so bad with gout that I can hardly hold my pen.

Your's very sincerely

C. Poulett Thomson

P.S. I have taken Grey and I have no doubt I shall give him plenty to do.

Montreal May 28, 1840

My dear Lord John.

The gout has got into my right hand so I must use another's to write to you, and must put my mark to the despatches, not inappropriate to this province.

I have your two letters of 30th April by the B. Queen, I think I understand what you are at with the clergy reserves, and I suppose it will end in your having brought in a new bill for the settlement.[85] I must own I think the bolder course would have been the best, if, as seems probable, there is no legal defect in the bill except what relates to the act of 1827. You had ample precedent for this course in the Canada tenures act. Pray refer to Lord Ripon's despatches of the 31st January and 25th May 1831. He not only obtains power to enable the King to assent to an act of the Canada legislature avowedly illegal, but obtains it and uses it when he declares, in the same despatch, that the bill is neither just in itself, nor efficient with a view to the objects contemplated by its authors. Really after this for Goody[86] to get up and accuse me of having assisted in passing an illegal act was a stretch of impudence, and I think it was hardly fair in Lord Melbourne not to have given me more support in reply, especially as I have stated to you in a despatch, when I sent home the bill, that it did most probably infringe the imperial act of '27 and that it would be necessary to remove the difficulty. I had written a despatch upon the whole of this subject but as I think there is perhaps a little too much gout in it, I have reserved it till I see the result of what you do. You must of course be best able to judge on the spot what will carry Ellenborough and Ashburton with you, and therfore if you have adopted as I conclude the second course instead of the first you will not have done so without good reason. But I tremble for any new bill in the Lords which has to go to details: under the first course they must have taken or rejected the whole, and I think they would have been afraid to do the last; under this they may cut and carve as they please, and in a way very unsuited to Canadian palates.

Remember one thing; that if there be any attempt to give the Church of England a superiority in point of station, or title, or tenure of property, five sixths of the province will never submit to it, and you will have the most loyal and the most stirring part of the population, the Scotch, united to a man against you.

Arthur was so frightened at this idea that he wrote to me after the arrival of the Grt. Western offering to go home in order to convert the Bishop of London.

You seem to think that the N. American provinces and their capitals be as near each other as Downing Street to the Parks, when you tell me to move off to Halifax to go and settle matters there. I will go there however if I possibly can manage it, because a particular account from thence may enable you to act with more decision and with less appearance of harshness to either party, but I shall be very much surprized if the result of my visit leads me to offer you any other advice than I have already done; to send out a sensible civil government (sic) who will manage the assembly and Mr. Howe too. When people have got personally irritated against each other, you cannot expect to come back to that exercise of forbearance and discretion on either side which are essential to going on smoothly. After all it is a storm in a puddle and not worth neglecting any of the greater interests of these colonies to set right.[87]

I hope Palmerston will have sent over his propositions to the Yankees by the next steamer at latest. Fox[88] has not been able to do anything yet for a provisional arrangement and I have no doubts will not until the British proposition is before the President—then, I dare say that the plan I mentioned to you before can be effected, which would be an extremely good settlement. In the meantime, there are some rumours here that the Americans mean to replace the civil posse in the forts, by military. Into this I have enquired, for, should it be done without a fresh understanding with us, I should consider it such a change in the status quo, as would justify me in erecting a block-house at the Little Falls and sending some men to the Madawaska settlements.

The Solicitor General Andrew Stuart, a brother of the chief justice, died a few weeks ago. I have made a new one, Mr. Day the best I could get. I hope he will do; and he is at least sure of a seat in the Union parliament—pray send me his warrant. Pray let me have my lawyer without any delay, le Marchant must pack him off.

Adieu I am now in my sixth week of gout, and the last is worse than the first, if it goes on, you will have to get a new Governor General, expecially if you want an ambulatory one.

Ever my dear Lord John
Yours very truly
C. POULETT THOMSON

GOVT. HOUSE MONTREAL 27 June, 1840[89]

PRIVATE

MY DEAR LORD JOHN

I have closed my Special Council, and I send you home my ordinances. They have done their work extremely well, thanks to Stuart and my new Solicitor General who turns out admirably, & thanks too to the Atty. Genl.[90] having been confined to his bed for the last two months, for he does me more harm than good, being the worst Lawyer in the Province, and always getting me into blunders.

I have passed some, tho' not all, the measures which are indispensable previous to the Union.[91] The Registry Bill still remains, but that I shall get thru' in the autumn after it has been for two or three months before the Public, which was the course I adopted with the Judicature Bill and found most advantageous. Education also stands over, but it is impossible to do anything in that until we get the municipalities erected in the districts.

I am sorry that you would not make the alteration I wished in the Schedule of the Union Bill but it does not much signify, I am happy to find. I shall bring the Judicature Bill into operation at the time fixed for it, and the Special Council will provide in the first instance for the Salaries. When Parlt. meets the United Legislature will then make the altered appropriation as required by the Bill without any difficulty, I entertain no doubt; tho' I still think it would have been far better not to have compelled the agitation of the subject in the first session, when it might so easily have been avoided. Of the benefits to flow from this Bill, and especially from that establishing Sheriffs' Courts it is impossible to speak too highly. They are in fact, both of them, as well as some other measures which have been passed, indispensable preliminaries to the Union, and I would never have recommended the adoption of that measure for Lower Canada, and certainly would never consent to take the responsibility of bringing it into operation so early, but with the thorough understanding that such measures as these were previously to be enacted, thus preparing the country for a return to an Assembly, when owing to the ignorance and unfitness of those, even the best among them, who will compose it, works of this kind of a most enlarged and comprehensive character, and at the same time involving details and personal & national feelings would stand no chance.

I am glad you have adopted my other suggestions in the Union Bill, altho' you would not take that relating to the Judges or the Changes on the Civil List. With regard to this last, how I am to pay 5,450£ pensions to which the faith of the Crown stands pledged when the Bill declares that only 5,000£ shall be thus allotted, is more than I can tell! Perhaps you will point out a mode. And I shall be in great difficulty with regard to offices abolished under the Union. It is very easy for you to say "Surely you can do with 75,000£ Civil List." To be sure I could! But you have placed all sorts of conditions upon the appropriation, and they are what will hamper me and do the mischief.

You have certainly been very fortunate hitherto with the Bill and I am delighted to find that so little objection has been taken in Parlt. to my scheme. The additional members I care nothing about—They are only absurd —but what else can you expect to get when you take Ellice's[92] advice or believed what he says? I see that he told you Sherbrook was "a *town* of great importance." It is a village in the woods, and may have *ten qualified* voters perhaps. As far as the Govt. is concerned such places as Cornwall, Niagara, Sherbrook, & Byetown are an advantage. I shall [illeg.] all the four members from my drawing room. But it will raise an outcry against close Burroughs and give causes for an early demand for a change.

I hear rumors however of a far more important line of mischief being meditated by the Bear, with the aid of Peel, who from knowing nothing of the subject may perhaps be misled. I allude to the rejection of the municipal Clauses. If this were really to be done, Ellice will have defeated the Union Bill quite as effectually as if his opposition had succeeded last year; and have recalled me as much as he wished to do by his letter to the Morning Chronicle. The establishment of Municipal Govt. by Act of Parlt. is as much a part of the future scheme of Govt. for the Canadas as the Union of the two Legislatures, and the more important of the two. Last year, as a Member of the Cabinet I would never have consented to the Union without that condition being coupled with it. It was made a necessary condition in my instructions, and I should consider the abandonment of it as fatal to the measure. The establishment of good local Govt. is an undertaking far beyond the scope of a Colonial Legislature and never could be obtained from it in a good shape or until after years of discussion; and all chance of good Govt., in Lower Canada especially, depends on its immediate adoption. But I cannot believe it possible. Still I am very nervous till I hear the fate of the 3d reading, for every one here who has heard the report is panic-struck.

I like your Clergy Reserves Bill very much. God speed it thru' the House of Lords! Your alterations giving the distribution of the Church of England share to the Society, and that doing away with the periodical census, are improvements on my Bill, which I would have carried if I could, but failed. Their introduction by *you* will do no harm. But I trust the Catholics may not be excluded. The *Protestants* will gain nothing by it for twenty years, for there will be nothing to divide beyond the present charges, and the Catholics will lose nothing which they have at present, as that is secured to them under the third head of sec. 56 of the Union Bill. But it will be felt as an act of great injustice and hardship by all, and it will entirely alienate the most loyal body of men in the Province. It will give occasion for endless complaint of the present charges being paid by the Province, and of course there is no other fund from which it can come. It is in fact a needless insult—of no practical benefit to its authors, and injuring not the interests, but only wounding the feelings, of those against whom it is directed.

You will have seen that I long ago let out Mr. Viger, and that I *un*-suspended the Habeas Corpus. I hope you will have let Joseph Hume[93] know that I did both long before he opened his mouth about either.

Ever Your's sincerely

C. POULETT THOMSON

[P.S.] I am very much obliged to you for having set me right with the House respecting, the legality of my Clergy Reserves Bill, when you brought in your's.[94] It is what Lord Melbourne ought to have done when I was attacked by Abinger[95] and Goody.

GOVT. HOUSE MONTREAL 28 *June* 1840

PRIVATE

MY DEAR LORD JOHN.

Thank you for your letters of the 29th May and 3r June. I will enquire into the matter alluded to in the first when I get to the Upper Province. I believe that the Short Hills Gentlemen were a set of the greatest scoundrels in the world and richly deserved hanging.[96] But I will see about them.

I am sorry that Palmerston does not like my plan of employing the military only in the disputed territory. Instead of their leading to the establishment of Posts and Blockhouses and settlement, they will afford the only means of preventing these things. What took place last year under his Civil Posse? Besides you cannot, even if it were desirable, confine the Yankees to a Civil Posse and not yourselves; and then what will you do with your posts at Temisquata & along the St. John's, withdraw your troops and leave your communication with the Lower Provinces undefended? I wish he would consider what this Civil Posse on the Yankee side is. It is not a set of Constables with Staves. It is a body of men as well armed and quite as effective for the warfare of the woods, nay more so, than any regular troops, but withall a reckless set of fellows without control of any kind and no responsible commander. It is this control & responsibility which you would get from the Regulars. Take care that in grasping the shadow, you do not lose the substance. As soon as Maine can get credit for another shinplaister([illeg.] Bank note) or get up a little sympathy again, she will take the matter out of the hands of the Central Govt., go ahead again with Roads, land sales & block houses, until she involves us in a collision, when the general Government *must* support her. You must not treat the American Govt. as you would any European State—and if you miss this opportunity of getting the Washington People fairly pledged and Maine altogether removed from any means of interfering, it will not again occur.

I have written you a despatch on this subject[97] in order to send you one I wrote to Fox, and record my opinions. I presume that Palmerston will have sent him some instructions on this point, and under the view which he takes, I shall of course do nothing till I hear further from you.

Fox and Sir R. Jackson both entirely agree with me. By the bye, you sent me the Commissioners Report, but *not* the map, and it is unintelligible without it. Will you direct it to be sent?

I have recovered nearly from the gout, but the fit has been a terrible one—Tomorrow I go to Quebec and thence I hope directly to Halifax, for I want to get back to Upper Canada where my presence is really important. It will be sharp work to get it into the summer, but I must try, as the Elections all depend on my going up. You will have written I hope to Halifax on the 1st July, not to New York.

I don't see, so far as my accounts go, when or how your Session is to end, but I suppose it will as usual, half the bills bucked in the Lords. I wish Baring joy of having got thro' his taxes so smoothly, tho' I wish he had not spoilt his argument for them by calling them *permanent*. In that sense they would be the worst he could have proposed—[illeg.] plan over again—To supply a *temporary* deficiency they are the best.

You have indeed had hard work, and I anxiously enquire about you from every arrival who has had any opportunity of seeing you. I trust that you will get thro' physically as well as you have done morally. I am sorry to find

Howick and Charles Wood deserting you on Stanley's Bill.[98] The first excuses himself to me, but I have told him that I can see no justification. It was not a point of principle—only of discretion—but his temper did it. I suppose you are now safe for the session; so at least Billy Holmes writes to me in introducing somebody or other, and he writes but despondingly of his party's prospects if they did get you out.

Ever, My dear Lord John

Your's Most Truly

C. POULETT THOMSON

Amidst his work and worries, Thomson was disturbed by the delay and apparent neglect in securing for him the promised peerage.

GOVT. HOUSE MONTREAL 28 June 1840

CONFIDENTIAL

MY DEAR LORD JOHN

I write you one line on my personal affairs in consequence of what you say in yours of 3d inst.

I have *no* letter from Lord Melbourne by the Gr. Western, which however, if it was what you tell me, another put off, I do not regret. But I think his conduct in the business most unfair and almost insulting to me. The Queen's pleasure taken some months ago, as I was informed by yourself—the very ridiculous difficulties with regard to the title for which alone, I was informed he waited, removed—and now a fresh delay.

I have borne this hitherto from the wish to do nothing which could annoy you, or injure the Public service, but I can submit to it no longer especially as it is now matter of remark that I should apparently have performed my business well, and have no testimony to this being felt at home—People begin to doubt that I have satisfied the Queen or the Govt., and I cannot either forbear contrasting this delay in the redemption of a solemn pledge to me with the speed with which honors have been conferred on others.

I must beg you therefore, if Lord Melbourne still delays, to allow me to return home at once. The business which I engaged to do is done as you admit beyond your expectations, and at home I may at least enquire whether the Queen's pleasure has been reversed and take my own course.

I do this with regret, but under my feeling I can do no otherwise.

I hope to receive an answer upon my return from Halifax as it will decide my going to Upper Canada, and I am sure you are too just not to give me one as soon as possible.

Ever my dear Lord John
Your's Most truly
C. POULETT THOMSON

CHAPTER IV

In Nova Scotia the lieutenant-governor, Sir Colin Campbell, had long been involved in a political and constitutional conflict with the reformers led by the redoubtable Joseph Howe. As governor-general the duty devolved upon Thomson to go thither to end this strife. He arrived in Halifax July 9th and soon reported *veni, vidi, vici.*

HALIFAX 27*th July* 1840[99]

PRIVATE

My dear Lord John

I have put matters quite right for you for the present in Nova Scotia. Mr. Howe has made the amends honorable and eschewed his heresies on Responsible Govt. publicly in his newspaper,[100] and except a few old women, without the slightest influence in the Colony, by whom Sir Colin Campbell has been surrounded, all is peace and harmony. I read people, parties, Assembly and all a good lecture in an answer I gave to an address of which I hope you will approve—at least the people here do so as fully as I could wish, and I have not the least doubt that there is no colony in the British Dominions which can be governed more easily than this.

I have told you in a dispatch as fully as I can in such a document[101] the causes of this mighty storm in a puddle, and the mode I have taken to quell it, as well as what I recommend to be done. But the plain English of the whole is that Sir Colin Campbell is utterly unfit to govern a Colony of this kind, and partly from temper & partly from utter ignorance of Civil Govt. has brought all this mess upon you & himself. There are no *parties* here before the Public in the way we understand them, or as they exist in Canada. At least five sixths of the Assembly care nothing about Politics, and think only of their Roads and Bridges. There are half a dozen men of some ability on both sides many even of whom he has alienated instead of using, whilst all of them were to be had with the greatest ease. The man who was the leader of the Govt. party as it is termed and was the mouth-piece of the Executive quitted the Council some months ago, because as he told me himself there was *no Government*. Unlike other Colonies on this side the Atlantic, the Crown officers are excellent men here—liberal and popular—but no power was given them, and their advice neither taken nor even sought. Mr. Howe, a very good kind of man, clever, active, and even by his opponents admitted to be honest and manly, carefully excluded and affronted. So that in the assembly the Governor has lately possessed not even one solitary friend to stand up for him or effect **to do the Govt. business.**

In this state of things it is not surprising that the Assembly ran riot, or that the disappointed ambition of a few individuals led them into extreme measures.

But I have calmed all this for the present. The Leaders on both sides, I mean of course the Parliamentary Leaders, for I can recognize no others, are perfectly satisfied with my recomposition of the Council and I should have proceeded to carry it into effect myself, if I had not found the people perfectly reasonable, and willing to wait. This however being the case, I have thought it best to do nothing for the moment, and to leave you the opportunity of sending out directions to Sir Colin Campbell to make the changes I have proposed, or of dispatching another Governor to do so. Sir Colin does not offer objection to any of them, except Mr. Huntingdon[102] (sic) to whom after all he has no personal dislike, but he has got some story of his having been heard to wish success to Papineau in 1838. He however is an influential man in the party and ought to be appointed. Mr. Young[103] was personally disagreeable to him, and of course I wd. *not* propose him.

Whether you determine however on sending out these instructions to Sir Colin, or on dispatching another Governor, the sooner it is done the better. If there is any delay in the last, then let the instructions come out to Sir Colin directly—and perhaps that may be the best way of letting him down easily.

But another Governor you *must* have in the course of the autumn and before the new Elections, for even with the Council which I propose for him, Sir Colin Campbell can afford no chance of any permanent tranquility or of the system being fairly worked out. He is not only incompetent to Civil Govt., but is too much mixed up with personal & party feelings.

I say this with great reluctance because I like him extremely. He is a fine bobspirited Highlander, hospitable and thoroughly honorable—wishing well to the Colony —but it is the truth. His character however may be perfectly saved by your sending a Civilian (the only man you ought) and by your declaring that it is not any longer your intention to allow the Commander of the Forces to govern the Colony. It is a great pity by the bye, that you did not make him Commander in Chief in B.N. America; for that he would have done extremely well; and if Sir R. Jackson comes home, of which I hear a rumor, you might remove him there.[104]

I have been greatly struck by the contrast between this Govt. and New Brunswick, where Harvey certainly found a much worse state of things than existed here. All is peace and harmony there—and entirely owing to his good management. He has by dint of *blarney* and conduct combined got his Govt. into better order than any other on this continent, and if he would never *write* a line, would be the Pearl of Civil Governors.

I have not received a line from you by the Britannia, the Halifax Steamer—and my dispatches by the British Queen have not reached me so I am in total darkness as to the fate of the Union Bill, except that I see by the Papers of the 3d July that the Duke[105] had declared against it. If however, as I also gather from the Papers (*tho' I cannot believe it*), the plan for local Government has been abandoned by you, it is to be hoped that the Duke may have thrown out the Bill. The Union is impossible without that part of the scheme, and would only do the greatest mischief. I suppose that I shall now only learn all this by the Gt. Western, when I get to Upper Canada whither I shall go the week after next. Tomorrow I embark for Quebec.

Believe me ever
Your's very truly,
C. Poulett Thomson

Leaving Nova Scotia Thomson spent two days with Sir John Harvey in New Brunswick and then travelled through the eastern townships of Lower Canada. On August 19th he left Montreal for a tour of Upper Canada.[106]

Drummondville 28, Aug. 1840

PRIVATE

My dear Lord John

I have not a line from you as my dispatches by the Steamers are missing and I am therefore entirely in the dark respecting all your proceedings, except indeed that I have received the Union Act, *without* the clauses for the local Govt. I have already told you my opinion of this—that I had much rather have had the Bill deferred, for I defy you to govern these Provinces without such a system, & you have by the abandonment of its enactment by Parliament thrown away not only the opportunity of securing good Government in the Canadas, but also the prospect of obtaining it by the same means thro' the Legislatures of the Lower Provinces.[107] Till I hear from you, of course I can decide on nothing however. But whatever becomes of me, I shall deplore to the end of my life the weakness of the Govt. in thus throwing away the means of making these fine Provinces contented & of establishing a Constitution under which their affairs could be safely and properly administered—and all, so far as I can see, to please a man whose ignorance of all Canadian matters is only to be exceeded by that of the unfortunate dupes to whom he has sold his property for ten times its value, and who has never ceased his opposition to the Union and to every measure of mine.[108]

I am here in the mean time on my road to Lake Erie and the upper part of the Province—a tour which will probably occupy me a fortnight before I get to Toronto which I did not visit on my way up, and altogether occupy three weeks before my return to Montreal. So you will not hear from me till the next Steamer which will leave New York on the 1st Oct., unless indeed I can get dispatches off by some liner in the interim.

I have been every where extremely well received; in the Townships with enthusiasm—and very well in the Upper Province. I filled up my corporations at Quebec and Montreal to the satisfaction of *all* parties, rather a feat in this divided country, and I have no doubt of doing the same by the District Courts and the other appointments, if I am here to make them.

With such a prospect to have it all ruined to please that rascally Bear is too bad. He has had the impudence to write me eight sheets of paper by the bye, in almost every line of which there is a blunder of the grossest character.

By the bye he must have misled *you*, begging your pardon, unless you are misreported in the newspapers which have made you say that the Townships in Upper Canada possessed the power of taxation, and that the Court Houses & Gaols, etc., were erected by those means. I have told you, and Lord Durham explained over and over again that with an admirable machinery of officers, the Townships possessed no power of taxation whatever and indeed no power at all.

But I shall have to write to you fully upon the whole of this subject whenever I get your letters, so I must not now go into it.

I have been unwell again from fatigue, but a few days rest at this place have patched me up for the moment.

Sir George Arthur who is here, is willing to stay on till the Union is proclaimed, which cannot under any circumstances be done till after Xmas, and when it is, the Gov. Gen'l. can secure a deputy in either Province in which he may be wanted, so there will be no occasion for a new Lt. Governor. The man who is west in command of the troops in U.C. is utterly unfit and Clitherow[109] or Macdonald (sic)[110] who probably wd. come up to command if Sir George went away equally so. There will be a difficulty the less therefore by his staying.

Ever my dear Lord John
Your's very sincerely,
C POULETT THOMSON

[P.S.] The newspapers contain *four* gazettes since the assent was given to the Union Bill, & I see nothing of my Peerage. I suppose Ld. Melbourne means to go the whole hog in promise breaking. So be it—but it is really a little too bad.

TORONTO 16 *Sept.* 1840

PRIVATE

MY DEAR LORD JOHN

I received at Port Colborne on Lake Erie your dispatches by the Acadie and your letter of the 3d. Augt. but in neither a word of explanation on the subject of the Municipal Clauses. That the Union Bill is ruined by their rejection I need not repeat, and if I yielded to temper, or did what I believe my due to my own reputation or your's either, as the parties responsible for the working of the Bill, I should defer carrying it into operation. However *you* seem to think otherwise, and therefore I feel bound after mature reflexion to try to go on the best way I can and I will stay and meet the first Parliament, subject of course to your undertaking to defend the course which I have determined upon, namely that I shall establish a kind of local Govt. by the Special Council in Lower Canada, & propose the adoption of the general measure in Upper Canada, to the United Legislature. I have stated all this fully in a dispatch in order that it may appear on record. As an honest man, I cannot proclaim the Union in Lower Canada without the assistance which some Local Government and the establishment of some Govt. authority in different districts will alone afford the Executive; and without it too, all those measures which I have passed in that Province for District Courts, Stipendiary Magistrates, Police, Prisons etc. would fall through, for they are all based upon the supposition that this part of the Union Bill would have been persevered in. I suppose indeed you must have intended something of this kind by that *wonderful* clause 58 which no human being, layman or Lawyer can understand the meaning of.

I confess that I have not arrived at this determination without considerable difficulty, for however I may patch the thing now, the opportunity of effectually setting to right the Constitutions of all the Colonies in North America is lost, and with it nearly every chance of good government in the Canadas especially. But I have been determined by two considerations. One, that *you* have stood by me most gallantly & have supported all my plans (however abandoned I have been in the House of Lords)—the other, that my late "progress" has satisfied me that I have obtained now that hold over the People and over parties in the Colony, that no new man could acquire. So I will set to work, tho' I do so with a very faint heart and the most bitter regret at the lost opportunity.

Dowling and Stuart will have the ordinances for the Local Councils & Townships, and for the other measures which remained over in June, ready by the beginning of next month and I shall pass them at once and then close my Special Council. I shall proclaim the Union for the new year or rather for the 5th Jany, which will suit the winding up of the Finances of the Two Provinces and of the Crown Revenues, and I shall have the Elections immediately afterwards if possible. Elections can only take place in this country before November or after the Snow Roads are established, because people can't move in that interval. I shall write to you from Montreal, where I can get legal advice, about the Commissions & the Council. I think you see difficulties which do not at all exist. As far as I understand the matter you have nothing to do but to send over a Commission appointing me Governor of the United Province which I open when

I have proclaimed the Union, & swear myself in before any body you may appoint in the Instructions. I then appoint my Executive Council which requires *no* confirmation to enable the Members to act—and the Legislative Council will be recommended afterwards in the usual way by me & get their Mandamus from home in time for the opening of Parliament or even for its being summoned, which is all that is necessary. Certainly I should not think of declaring publicly in the Colony who are to be the *Legislative* Counsellors (sic) before Parlt. are summoned.

I have made a most successful "progress" and have satisfied myself that I can beat both the Ultra Tories and the extreme Radicals at the Elections in Upper Canada. I cannot suppose that you will read the fifty or sixty addresses which I shall have to send you home when I get back, but the same spirit pervades the whole of them, confidence in my Govt. and a determination to support me; and I believe that they mean what they say. In Lower Canada it is a different matter—there, the spirit of the old House of Assembly is again at work and many of the French Members will be the same, or if not the same men, with the same spirit as before. Witness Mr. La Fontaine's address which you will have seen I suppose. But I shall have 16 or 18 English or good French Canadian members out of their quota & these with the Upper Canadians will do, especially when I get them into the Upper Province.

I have no longer the slightest doubt about Kingston as the seat of Government, but I am much afraid that I cannot patch up a place there to meet in in the Spring —but I return there in two or three days and if I can

make use of a large store and other buildings belonging
to the Navy which are now merely used for barracks,
I shall do so. If not, I must go to this place, but that will
be very inconvenient. Nothing however would make me
meet in the Lower Province or hold the central Govt.
there.

I really had no notion of what Upper Canada is till
I made this tour. I always thought that the country
was a fine one, but the whole of that tract of land lying
between the three Lakes and nearly as large as England
is unsurpassed in any part of the world, I believe, and
any one district of it contains more real wealth & intelli-
gence than all Lower Canada (exclusive of the townships).

I hope to get the letters by the British Queen at
Kingston—and to hear of your house being up at last.
I am delighted by the Quadruple Treaty. It will bring
Louis Phillippe (sic) to his bearings and as for all the
bluster of the French, it will only make them ridiculous.

Believe me, my dear Lord John

Your's most truly

C POULETT THOMSON

[P.S.] I must wait to see your Clergy Reserve Bill
when it gets thro' the Lords, but in the mean time I have
been preaching peace and quiet to the People about it
and I hope that I have succeeded. Your expression that
there was "no Superiority" has helped me well with the
Scotch who are however furious at having been *jockeyed*
out their fair share. Their members are in *fact* almost,
if not quite equal to those of the Church of England,
only in many of the returns made by the Clerks of the
Peace of the Kirk people were disguised as "Presby-

terians," and in others as belonging to "the Church of Scotland" and then in the returns sent home, the former were classed as Dissenters and as *not* belonging to the true Kirk. You will have all this out in a solemn protest, but I hope to persuade them to content themselves with that & not to agitate. If you will give Egerton Ryerson what I have asked and what is perfectly just, *I* will keep him quiet when he gets back, but I must have that to do it. I am in the greatest favor with the Upper Canadian Methodists, so a fig for Mr. Alder and the English Conference.

The desire for a peerage was at last fulfilled.

MONTREAL 27*th Sept.* 1840

PRIVATE

MY DEAR LORD JOHN,

I received your's of the 28 Augt. from Scotland on my way down the Ottawa on Thursday last the 24th. So I see Melbourne has made me Lord *Sydenham*. As I have no letter from him or from my Brother about it, I don't know who was my Godfather or why I was thus baptised. But I can't say that it is a matter of the least consequence to me and the adjunct of Toronto pleases the people of the Upper Province immensely. My opinion of the whole transaction remains just as it was, and is strengthened by the conclusion, tho' at least it has had this advantage as far as *I* am concerned, that I have gone my whole tour, and have received the really wonderful declaration of confidence and support from the vast body of the People of the Provinces given to myself, without any apparent aid or countenance from H.M.'s

Prime Minister. The People of Montreal too, I am happy to say, are now chiming in with their Upper Canadian Neighbors—they are slow to learn, but they have yielded to the practical conviction of better roads, better streets, Quays building—Police cheaper and yet more efficient—Justice well administered by a Police magistrate instead of a set of ignorant Unpaid—A Corporation to manage their own matters—and the public servants made to work—besides the general measures, which I have given them in common with the Province and which they are now beginning to understand. So they determined on giving me a great public entry, but the Gout seized me at Kingston, and I was obliged to decline it. As for the French nothing but time will do anything with them. They hate British rule—British connexion—improvement of all kinds whether in their Laws or their roads. So they sulk, and will try, that is, their Leaders, to do all the mischief they can. However that will not be much, for the Habitans (sic) altho' they are daily crammed with the most absurd stories by these People, have suffered so much by the former disturbances that they will not again make the slightest movement. Before the Union is finally proclaimed a thoroughly good system of law and Govt. will have been established for the Province, and that in time will work, I trust, a more improved state of things as well as of feelings.

My letters will have told you what I shall do about the local Government here. The argument which you say has some force, viz. that the Priest and the Lawyer of the village might counteract the Assembly tells just the other way, and only shows how entirely unacquainted

People are in England with the real state of things. The Priest and the Lawyer return the member *now* and *that* without any control, or upon any ground except hatred to the English Govt. and the English name. Establish a field in which the Inhabitants can discuss their own interests, and parties will soon be split in the different parishes and districts, and set there some one in the confidence of the Govt. who will expose the misrepresentations which are made, and you will either get different members, or have a good check upon them. I have not hitherto failed in anything I have undertaken on this side the water, and if you will only support me in what I do under the powers I have, I may yet get over the difficulties that the Union Act, as it has been passed, has created. If you will not—of course I must leave it to somebody else to try. But in the mean time I shall go on my own way.

I hope by the bye, that except for the Financial settlement for which of course you must go to Parliament, you will not have occasion to mention the word "Canada" next session. I am sure that it will be better both for this Province and Parlt.; for the discussions there do no good here, and certainly do not raise the character of that august assembly. On the other hand what *you* have done by *your* vigorous administration of all Canada matters in Downing St. is immense. You have done more by your ready and prompt acquiescence in the reduction of Postage to attach the People to the Mother Country than was ever before effected—and tho' Parlt seems to have refused it's assistance to the Tea duties, the intention on your part has told well. By the bye I wish Labouchere[111] wd. tell me the meaning of this matter—the result is that we shall lose ten or fifteen thousand pounds for the year, and smuggling go on more than ever. I never saw during my tour a leaf of anything but smuggled Tea.

Thank you for your permission to settle the matter of the Wesleyans. I shall send directly for my high Priest, and so cool him down upon the Reserves. The Scotch I have in hand. Since I left Toronto, I have had a meeting with their principal Lay Leaders and shall keep them quiet.

I was very glad to see you date from Scotland tho' your stay there was so short. You must indeed have been fagged at the end of the session in which I was sorry to observe you seemed to have little assistance! I always told [you] you were buying Punch in Macaulay.[112] Labouchere seems the only one who has occasionally given you help, which I expected and am very glad of. But your Lords seem worse than ever. What is Clarendon[113] about that he has not come out? The Canada question was just one to make his Parliamentary fortune by, instead of leaving to Ellenboro the distinction of being the only Peer who had ever read or heard, or knew anything of the matter. The Duke of Wellington discovering that *I* had raised the cry for responsible Govt. and Ld. Melbourne finding out an *Island* in the St. Lawrence called William Henry or Sorel!!!

I cannot believe that the French will run their heads against the walls so much as to go to war, but certainly Mahomet Ali will do all he can to get them into one. However I rejoice at your treaty.

I will write to Falkland[114] and give him the best advice in my power. I am sure that nothing can be easier than to govern that Colony. I am sorry to tell you that Sir

George Arthur had a serious attack of paralysis after he left me at Drummondville and I had settled with him to stay till the Union was proclaimed; and I found him at Toronto so weak and so likely to suffer from any excitement of business that his medical men recommended his getting away as soon as possible. Under these circumstances, if he has *not* heard from you by the Britannia of which I can get here no information, I shall write to him urging him to go without waiting. Either Macdonald or Clitherow will go up from here to command the troops, and tho' neither could be trusted to do *anything* in Civil Govt., I believe that either may, to do nothing but what the Secretary who is an excellent man will tell them. So I shall manage to get on, & certainly want no one from England for the two or three months that will remain. Poor Sir George! I should be very sorry if the finale of his Govt. proved fatal to him, and that is what his Physicians and Lady Arthur seem to apprehend from his staying.

I have got the gout again I am sorry to say, but in the feet.

Ever your's most truly

SYDENHAM

GOVT. HOUSE MONTREAL 12 *Oct.* 1840

PRIVATE

MY DEAR LORD JOHN

I have scarcely anything to say and write a line only that the mail may not go without one to you. En revanche you will have a host of dispatches, the necessary consequence of my tour, which has put my official correspondence in arrears.

If you have not already done so, write to Sir George Arthur to bring him away. I am afraid he will kill himself there, & I don't want that on my conscience.

Things go on very well here and the accounts from the Upper Province are all I can wish. My measures will be ready for the Special Council very soon and I shall have them together to pass them. There will be a vast deal to do however before the Union, or at least before the Parlt. can meet, in the entire reconstruction of offices as well as in carrying into effect the different things required by the Act to be done before that can be summoned—Limits of Towns, etc., etc. So you must not be impatient. The rump of the old assembly will give me a great deal of trouble, but I shall beat them. The worst of it is, that there really is not a French Canadian to whom it is possible to give an office.

I like the reports from your Emigration Board[115] very much indeed. They do not always know the particular *specialties* of this Land, and therefore I cannot always agree with them in details, but their general principles accord altogether with mine. I am sure that your establishment of this Board will do great good—in spite of that scamp Mr. E. G. Wakefield, who I suppose is angry that you did not put him there.

Pray make the Admiralty authorize the building another Steamer on Lake Ontario for which I have asked. It is of the utmost consequences to have a force on which we can call there.[116] We *could* hold that Lake —not so Lake Erie, out of which the Yankees would drive us at once.

I feel sure that your Eastern affairs will settle down without any French Gun-powder, tho' the Canadians

have got it about here, that the French are sending
20,000 men to Canada. I wonder how they would get
there! Sullivan's case in the Upper Province is a disagreeable one[117]—but I am quite sure that it is right to
pay him the sum I mention from the Crown funds which
can be easily done.

Ever my dear Lord John
Your's very sincerely,
SYDENHAM

GOVT. HOUSE MONTREAL 28 Oct. 1840

PRIVATE

MY DEAR LORD JOHN

Cunard's Steamer brought me your's of the
30th Sept. & 3d Oct.

I have written you a private letter, but separate in
order that you may make it official if you like, respecting
the land required at Kingston for military purposes. The
Ordnance conduct these matters on this Continent in
the most absurd way. Instead of buying the land they
may require, the moment their plan of defence is at all
digested, in which case it might probably be got for
10£ an acre, and if not wanted, afterwards sold again
at a large profit, they defer purchasing until the increase
of population and of commerce, so rapid in all Towns
here, has raised the value of the ground they want fifty
fold. This has been eminently the case at Kingston,
where ten or even five years ago they might have purchased all they want for a tenth part of what they must
now pay for it, and if they changed their plans and did
not make use of it, they might have resold it at a very
large profit—as any one with common sense, looking

only to the certain increase of trade and population at the place could have forseen. That however is past, and they must pay for their folly. But there will be now a just cause of increase in the value of the land they may want, and if they do not provide against it by instantly making their purchases, they will either have to suffer enormously, or to abandon altogether their plans. Hitherto not a soul suspects my intention of holding the Parlt. at Kingston and making it the seat of Govt.—on the contrary I have purposely discouraged the idea, in order to pick up for the Province the land which was necessary for Public buildings &c, in which I have just succeeded to my heart's content. But in six weeks or two months, it must be known, and then not an acre of the Glacis of your Redoubts, or the redoubts themselves will be to be had except at an advance of 2 or 300 %. I strongly recommend you therefore to direct the ordnance to close with Mr. Harkman [?] in England, (who has no Agent here authorized to sell) for the whole of his lot, and to instruct Col. Oldfield to buy without the least delay the rest that he wants. I cannot give him more than the time necessary to get an answer before I proceed with my operations publicly, but I will wait for that. Whatever the ordnance buy, whether they use it or not they can only gain by.

I look with great anxiety to your next accounts—it seems to me *next* to impossible that foolish people in France or England should prevail to the extent of really getting up a war, without as it seems to me the slightest motive—but your uneasiness alarms me. The reports of hostilities and a foolish mistake between Canada & Candia, in a declaration attributed to Admiral Roussin[118] have already had their effect here. These absurdities are circulated with inconceivable rapidity amongst the French Canadian population and a great deal of uneasiness prevails throughout the whole body. If the next accounts are more pacific, this will probably subside— if the reverse, there will, I have no doubt, be a good deal of excitement, but I apprehend no outbreak. I shall take, quietly, every precaution which seems to me necessary for what may arise. There is no absolute necessity to proclaim the Union before the 15 Feby and till then my despotic powers will continue in this Province, so that there will be ample time for any thing which may become necessary, as well as for seeing the result with you.

In Upper Canada everything is as I wish it, and in the English Counties here. From the French I expect nothing but trouble—the fact is they are unfit for representative Govt.—but if things are quiet in Europe, I do not mind anything they may do, and with time even they may be brought right.

Believe me, My dear Lord John
Ever your's most truly
SYDENHAM

MONTREAL 24 Nov. 1840

PRIVATE

MY DEAR LORD JOHN

I received by the Halifax mail of the 18th ult. your's of that date—the messenger with the mail of the 4*th* Nov. has not arrived tho' I just learn that the Caledonia had reached Boston. It is provoking, as my bag must go off tomorrow morning to be in time for her return.

I am very glad that you approve of my plans which have "progressed" so far satisfactorily. I have got a very good measure for Township officers and district Government before the Council which will pass in a few days when I shall proceed to carry it into effect without any delay. It is very popular with the Canadians except some of the very ultra Tories, and the Agitators amongst the French party who see that it will deprive them of power. Those latter however have not dared to abuse it much. But I have achieved, I hope, a much greater work even, by getting a Registry Bill,[119] the Pons Asinorum, as you know of Lower Canadian Legislation which is admitted to be the best ever produced and satisfies nearly all. It is a subject so interwoven with Old French law, and the habits of the people under it, that I do not profess to understand it, at least in it's details, but I have had the ordinance circulated for six weeks as widely as possible and invited objections and criticisms from all quarters—and the result has been nearly universal approbation. At all events therefore I am safe about it, and if there are any defects in the details the United Legislature may alter them. It is Stuart's work, who certainly is the most competent person perhaps in the world from his thorough knowledge of both French and English Law to have prepared the Bill.

So, if things go right here, and you have no war, I shall be able to keep pretty nearly to my dates for the union and the Elections.

I hope you will approve of my occupying the Madawaska Settlements. Indeed, under your instructions, I think I could do nothing else; but it is also the best thing. I dare say that they will growl about it at Washing-

ton but they will still be the more ready to come to some
understanding with us when they find that their scheme,
which I know to be to delay in order to gain point by
point upon us thro' Maine, is not successful. The only
thing I am afraid of is that Harvey who turns round in
24 hours should take it into his head not to keep the
troops—but I shall write to him plainly about this, for
it will not do to play the same foolish game as he did
last year.[120]

What an abominable mess the Horse Guards and
Macaulay have made of your Royal Canadian Regiment!
The best part of it is that the regulations are so absurd
that the Soldiers will not volunteer for it except a few
who do not understand them, or the worst people,
whom their officers persuade in order to get rid of them.
I have written you a dispatch about the *real* scheme,
which I hope will not be abandoned, & I shall send you
a plan shortly with calculations. I could not get Sir
Richard Jackson to write officially about the "conditions"
as he says his opinion was not asked by the Horse Guards
and he would not volunteer it, but he has sent home a
series of questions as to the right understanding of the
order, which demonstrate sufficiently their absurdity.

I cannot get from him yet the statement you required
in the summer of the military defences required for the
Canadas, so you must not complain of the delay. He sends
it in to me once a week and then begs to have it back
again.

I have got quite well again I am happy to say, tho'
I don't know what the winter will do. We have three feet
of snow already—but the navigation is still open. There
has been a great outcry about my making Mr. Wagner

the head of the Post office here a member of the Commission of enquiry, but as the Treasury ordered that one
of the Coms. should be an officer of the department,
I thought it best to take him rather than an inferior,
who would have been under his control, and been
afforded no responsibility. I made Dowling another—
so that we shall only have the Secretary to pay.

By the bye Dowling is of great service to me.

Ever my dear Lord John
Your's very sincerely
Sydenham

Montreal 24th Nov. 1840, 10 P.M.

PRIVATE

My dear Lord John
Since I wrote to you this morning, the messenger
has arrived bringing your dispatches and your letter to
me of the 31st ulto. There is nothing fortunately in the
former which will suffer from not obtaining an immediate answer. To the letter, I can reply at once.

I am extremely well pleased to keep Sir George Arthur
in Upper Canada till the Union is proclaimed; as he
stays, it appears, by his own desires, and clears my
conscience of the results to his health. He writes of late
that he is a great deal better, and can do his business as
usual. To say the truth, I should have been rather
frightened at Sir James MacDonald. He is such a Goose
as a Civilian. He is just now got into an absurd quarrel
with the People of Quebec about opening the gates of
the Town, in which I shall probably be obliged to
interfere and throw him over. Having kept the gate of

the farm at [illeg.] closed by main force, I believe he thinks that all gates ought hereafter to be kept shut too.

I am very much puzzled by your significant warning and precautionary advice. Surely, as regards the Public, you are stronger than ever. But of course I do not know what causes there may be within the Cabinet which may lead to a break up, and you probably would not have deemed it necessary to say anything on the matter without good reason. I hope however that it may prove otherwise, for I should regard *your* ceasing to hold office as the most serious calamity to the Country.

With regard to myself, your advice will be always nearly a law to me, and if the circumstances should unhappily arise, I should make almost any sacrifice of feeling or of opinion to conform to it. But I must say that I do not think my remaining here would then be attended with any advantage to the Public. Whatever success I have been able to obtain here I owe to my perfect reliance upon your friendship and your public character. Without a friend to consult, and obliged to rely entirely on my own judgment on all occasions, I have gone steadily forward with confidence because I have felt throughout that I could rely on your friendship to put the best construction on all that I did, and on your firm support and defence as a Minister and my Chief. But I should no longer feel the same confidence in any other, and my powers of being useful here would cease when any hesitation arose. With any one else, and above all with a Tory or Semi Tory administration, I should no longer feel myself the Minister for these Colonies, able to discuss matters with the Secretary of State on equal terms as if I was still his Colleague in the Cabinet, and satisfied that my opinion would have due weight—but I should have to weigh instructions to avoid responsibility—to hesitate where I now go boldly forward. In such a position I could be of little service. However, I will not anticipate and will repeat that whatever you wish or advise will have the utmost weight with me.

Whilst on this subject, I may as well add a word with regard to the more distant future. If all things go right with *you* at home, I consider myself pledged to meet the United Legislature, and carry them thro' their first session—but there my task ends. I shall then have got the vessel fairly under weigh and another Captain may command her just as well as myself. On public ground there will be an end of my mission. A regular Governor, and one who will take his usual term of service will do as well indeed better than I should—whilst on personal feelings, which I shall then be at liberty to consult, a Dukedom would not tempt me to stay. The life is the most intolerable that can be conceived. The parade and etiquette of it are diametrically opposed to all my taste and habits—their expense ruinous—and the climate most injurious to my health. As long as the thing *is* to be done, and I have work for eighteen hours out of the twenty four with the excitement of the job, I overlook all this—but when the machine is once well set a going and a regular Government established and at work, there will no longer be the least public necessity for my submitting to it any longer, and I may get my discharge. I thought to be sure that less time might have done this for me; however that can't be helped and I do not complain—but certainly next July or August must.

I told you all I had to say about affairs here in my

letter this morning. You seem to be getting thro' your Eastern affairs triumphantly.

I have been greatly shocked by poor Lord Holland's death. When shall we find his equal for amiable qualities and thoroughly liberal principles?

Ever your's very sincerely

SYDENHAM

PRIVATE

GOVT. HOUSE MONTREAL 20 Dec. 1840

MY DEAR LORD JOHN,

The messenger has as usual brought me your letter (of the 2d inst.) by the Boston steamer just as mine is starting to catch it on its' return—and thanks to the plaging (sic) alteration which the Treasury allowed Cunard to persuade them into of only *one* packet a month. I shall have no other opportunity of writing till Feby. I have sent you a dispatch about the Post Office arrangements. It is very provoking, when I have done so much to simplify the matter, and you and Baring have so greatly assisted, to have the authorities at St. Martin's Le Grand settling things all wrong, and producing discontent.

I wish you joy of your Princess Royal[121]—but still more of your Eastern Policy. Even the High Tories write in loud praise of it, and are compelled to confess that England never stood higher in the scale of nations, either for the power she has displayed, or the justice and moderation with which she has used it.

I am going on very quietly here in domestic matters— winding up my business with the Special Council and preparing for putting an end to it, and proclaiming the Union; tho' owing to the dilatoriness of the body, and the captiousness of Stuart, whose fault is that he can never be brought to cooperate with others, I do not advance so rapidly as I had hoped. The delay however is productive of good both here, and in the Upper Province. The violent party at Quebec are losing ground, and in the other Province asperities are daily softening down. The Tories see no hopes for themselves but in supporting the Government and the Ultra Rads are losing adherents. I am delighted that you have thrown over Stuarts crotchet about "the Governor General of all the Provinces" not being "Governor General of two."[122] I am obliged to send you a fresh mare's nest of his today, upon which I beg you to let me have the Law Officers' opinion without fail by return of the Steamer. He is so d——d obstinate when once he gets a thing into his head, that he would be capable of upsetting the whole of the ordinances passed since 1837 and prior to 1791 by a judgment from the Bench, on a case referred to him. All the Lawyers are dead against him which only makes him more pertinacious.

My township and district Councils ordinances are both passed, and so is my Registry Law, I am happy to say. By next mail I shall be able to send them—so that not a great deal now remains undone. I feel sure that you will like them.

By the bye let me warn you against Gillespie[123]—next to Ellice, I should say that he is the worst authority you can have upon Canadian matters. He knows nothing *himself*, and all the information he gets comes from Moffatt, the most pig headed, obstinate, ill tempered brute in the Canadas, now a member of the Special Council, but whom I shall certainly *not* put into the new Legislative Council.[124]

So much for my *home* matters—my Foreign affairs have given me infinite disturbance. Harvey has been playing exactly the same game that he did last year. After asking in the most pressing terms for a company to be sent to Madawaska, he has altered his mind completely, written to have them withdrawn, and worse than this, has told the Governor of Maine that he should do so, and entertained no doubt that I would consent —and this in the face of your positive instructions to him *not* to interfere. His object it seems upon "second thought" was to employ an "Armed Civil Posse" which I am pretty confident he possesses no power to do, and moreover has, if I am not mistaken the opinion of his Law Officers in his pocket, to that effect. I shall send you, if I can, copies of my correspondence with him, but at all events I must beg of you to repeat your injunctions to him contained in your dispatch of the 19th Feby 1840, that he is *not* to meddle in the Boundary question except under my directions. We owe the establishment of the Americans at the mouth of the Fish River entirely to his folly, and he will bandy fine sentences with General Scott,[125] or Governor Fairfield[126] whilst the yankees take possession and occupy the whole of the St. John's and our road to New Brunswick to boot. *They* understand his character perfectly and play on it unendingly. He talks of his dispatch to Governor Fairfield not committing *me*—as if he did not commit the Government of the Queen generally by what he does. It is impossible that I can go on, or take the responsibility of this business unless he is checked, and I am moreover convinced that the course which he now wishes to follow would be fatal to our obtaining a settlement. The valley of the Restook is fast settling with Yankees, and many are already on the St. John's—& all that is desired by the Maine People and even by the Presidential Govt. is, to be permitted quietly to continue those settlements, after which they will turn round and tell us we cannot dislodge "their People."[127]

I do not think that Harrison's [128] election will make much difference in this question. All parties are equally disposed to play the rogue. You will have had the opportunity of judging of the little truth there was in Van Buren's sentence in his message[129] upon the subject, for whilst he repeats his commonplace expressions of a desire to adjust the question, he knows full well that the point referred to England is one which we cannot yield, and is only put forward for delay. We must trust to numbers for driving them to some arrangement. If they see that they can no longer advance step by step till they have actually got the whole territory, they will agree to one —but until they are satisfied of that they never will.

You will find the subject of settlement along the St. John's referred to in my dispatch including the report on the defence of the Canadas, and *the Duke's* letter. I wish you would give me the means of settling a few hundred Emmigrants or others next summer. I would have the line surveyed by the ordnance in the Spring, and allotments made directly after, and I would get plenty of good people. But the good land is unluckily all to the South of the St. John's, and therefore settlement will be expensive. However, a line of road with good defences might be marked out, and then parties established to make it, and settle on it. Pray think of this, & give me some authority if you can. It would be money well spent.

Falkland seems to me to be going on very well, and my changes have answered perfectly. You will of course have directed him to keep Mr. McNab[130] in the Executive Council if he got into the Assembly, which he has done. Howe writes to me in great contentment and he and Falkland seem to agree well. In fact there is not the slightest difficulty in governing Nova Scotia, with only tolerable sense and conduct.

Believe me, my dear Lord John

Ever your's most truly

SYDENHAM

PRIVATE

MONTREAL 29 January 1841

MY DEAR LORD JOHN

I have just heard that the Horse Gds. wish Campbell whom I lately appointed to be my Military Secretary, to join his regiment the 7th Hussars now here, as he got his majority lately, which is the cause. Now there is nothing which could be so inconvenient or annoying to myself, or indeed to the Public Service as this.

I did not know Campbell when I took him in this country from Adam, but I made him an A.D.C. upon the character that I heard of him—& when Hall left, I appointed him at once Military Secretary. He is the *only* officer in these regions who can be of the least use to me, because he is the *only one* who has taken any pains to know the People & the Country; and at this juncture his loss would be most disastrous to me, as he manages the *Members* for me, both as to their Elections and their votes, and is the sole reliance I have.

I wish you to be good enough therefore to insist upon Campbell being left on my Staff till August next. His

Lt. Colonel being quite willing—a word from you to Lord Anglesey, the Colonel, putting it on political reasons would do—if the H. Gds. object.

But spare him till I have met my Parlt. I cannot.

I just catch the messenger.

Ever your's sincerely

SYDENHAM

The following despatch throws light on the financial situation in Canada and Sydenham's plans for handling it.

[*Copy*]

GOV. HOUSE MONTREAL 22 *Feby.* 41

CONFIDENTIAL

MY LORD,

The time is now approaching when it will become necessary for me to explain the extent of assistance towards the Financial Concerns of this Province which the Imperial Parliament may in its wisdom, and Generosity think fit to afford. On the opening of the United Legislature I am bound to make a statement to this effect, and it is besides indispensably required with a view to the arrangements which I shall be called upon to submit for the preservation of the public Credit of the Province, and the continuation of the great public works by which its prosperity can alone be assured.

In my despatch of the 27 June last, No. 129, I furnished a full and detailed statement of the financial situation of each Province, as well as an Estimate of the position which the Finances of the United Province would probably present after the Union. The only variation upon that Estimate, which the Experience of what has since

occurred offers, is, that on the one hand the Revenues
of the two Provinces have increased and may in my
opinion be therefore calculated as likely to produce ten
or fifteen thousand a Year more than I then reckoned
upon, even under the present system of taxation; and
on the other, the Debt of Upper Canada, has been
increased by about £100,000, by the Assent, which Her
Majesty has been advised to give to the Upper Canada
Act for buying out the private stockholders of the
Walland (sic) Canal. And that of Lower Canada, has
been augmented by the Loans authorized to be raised
within that province for different public Works to the
extent of £26,000. In this last case however the tolls to
be received will most undoubtedly cover, and eventually
pay off the sums borrowed, and the Province does nothing
more than lend its credit for the transaction, though I
regret to say that even with that double security, the
funds can only be raised at an interest of from 6 to 8
percent, and consequently at a heavy sacrifice.

H.M. Government have therefore the whole state of
our Finances distinctly before them. The total of debt
may be stated at about £1,325,000 Col. Stg. or £1,226,000
British Sterling.

That the Province of Canada possesses the most ample
means of paying, not merely the interest, but of refunding
the principal of this Debt, there can be no doubt whatever,
and I do not think it necessary to call upon the generosity
of the Mother Country to expend a single shilling, altho'
it would be easy to shew, that even if Great Britain were
to place at the disposal of the Provincial Govt. a sum
equal to the whole amount of its Debt; as a free gift, it
would be wise economy on its part, for the Imperial

Treasury can only obtain relief from the heavy expenditure which it is now annually called upon to incur within the province, equal nearly each Year, to that Amount, through the settlement of the domestic Affairs of the Colony, and by securing its prosperity, and the entire development of its natural resources.

But the assistance of the Mother Country is indispensable to enable Canada, either to support its present burthens, or advance in that Career which may render them light hereafter.

Nearly all the Canadian Debt has been contracted for Public Works which are begun but not completed, from which, when completed, a revenue will be derived, but which at the same time can only be rendered thus productive by fresh expenditure.

The province is sinking therefore under the weight of engagements which it can only meet by fresh outlay, whilst that very present inability to meet its Engagements, by destroying its credit, prevents it from obtaining the means for this expenditure, through which it can alone extricate itself permanently from its difficulties.

I can furnish no stronger illustration of this state of things, than the Welland Canal. The total outlay upon this work has been about £400,000 Curcy and I regret to say that it has been most improvidently and unwisely expended, owing to the wretched system which has been heretofore followed both with regard to money grants, and to the construction of Public Works by assistance from the Public Funds.

The Tolls, however of this Canal thus imperfectly made, which were in the Year 1838 about £6,000, and in 1839 about £12,000, have last year amounted to

£24,000—and would, I entertain not the slightest doubt amount to between £40,000 and £50,000—each Year, if the Canal can be kept open, and to a far larger amount hereafter. But unless a very considerable sum, can be raised, equal almost to that already expended, this great work must inevitably go to ruin, and this undertaking which is now the joint property of the Province, and of the Imperial Government, and might be made by fresh expenditure wisely conducted, amply to repay all that has been expended in it, will be irretrievably lost.

It would be idle however for the Canadian Government to attempt unassisted to obtain the necessary Funds. Its credit is unhappily so low that it cannot hope to do so, and even if it could find some Capitalists willing to undertake the operation, an exorbitant rate of Interest of 8 or 10 perCent, or an enormous sacrifice of Capital, by the sale of Debentures under Par, would destroy nearly all chance of its succeeding in a Commercial point of view.

I have given the Canal as an instance, but the same may be shewn to be the condition of nearly all the works for which the debt of the Province has been contracted. They are either in themselves, incomplete and consequently a dead weight, or rendered useless by the absence of other improvements necessary to make them productive.

It is in the power of Parliament alone, therefore, to afford the necessary assistance. What is required is such aid as shall at one & the same time diminish the Annual charge upon the Provincial Treasury for Debt already incurred, and by raising the Credit of the Province enable it to obtain the additional Funds, required to make its past expenditure productive, and I am satisfied that this may be done without the expenditure of a single shilling and with perfect security.

The plan which I was formerly authorized to propose namely the Guarantee of a Loan for Canada, to the extent of £1,500,000 would effectually secure both these ends.

I should propose therefore that the Treasury should be authorized to raise a Loan, to that Amount, the proceeds to be applied first to the liquidation at par of the Canadian Debt, and the residue for the completion of such public works as might be deemed expedient.

The Debt to be made a first charge upon Canadian Revenues, before all other Debt, if any afterwards be contracted by the Province, and to be specially provided for as such by the Canadian Legislature. All tolls or other securities which had been mortgaged, to the Province as security for the present debt to be made over in the same way. The Canada Stockholders to be compelled to receive their money at par, or New Stock, at a price proportionate to it.

No portion of the fund applicable to public Works, to be expended on any Work, which was not wholly and absolutely under the direction of the Executive Government, whether private stockholders had or had not any interest in the undertaking.

The advantage of this plan is two fold—First, by at once paying off the present Stockholders, the province would be relieved from an Annual Charge upon the whole debt of nearly 2 perCent, in as much as the rate of interest now paid is 5¾ perCent, whilst under the Guarantee of Great Britain the sum could probably be

raised at 3¾. And next that by these means, the stockholders would not be able to claim the unfair advantage
they would otherwise acquire from the greatly increased
marketable value which their Stock would undoubtedly
obtain, if the Credit of Canada generally were materially
raised, through the assistance in any other way of the
British Govt. as advantages they would have no right to.
The stockholders have it is true, a right, as will be found
set forth in paper Bb. of my despatch of the 27 June, not
to be paid off before certain fixed periods varying from
1842 to 1860, but on the other hand, their stock is not
even worth more than 75 or 80 for the 5 pCents, and
85 to 90 for the 6 perCents, if it be saleable at all, and
unless the Imperial Govt. interferes, will never again
probably be worth par. They will therefore be amply
compensated for this compulsion, tho' against the terms
of their bargain. Indeed, if H.M. Government consent
to propose this plan, I entertain little doubt that the
Chancellor of the Exchequer may not consider it unjust
to affix even a lower rate than par for the repayment
of the 5 perCent stock.

With regard to the residue of the loan, after redemption
of the debt, the plan which I suggest offers no less advantage, both to the Imperial Treasury, and to the province.

I have already stated that fresh outlay is indispensable
in order to render the Public Works productive. The
employment therefore of this portion of the whole Loan,
for this purpose affords additional security, that the
whole, both interest, and Capital will be repaid by the
Province, and at the same time by so greatly enhancing
the Credit of the Province, any further sums it may be
found necessary to raise, in order fully to complete the

works will be attainable at a low rate of Interest even upon Provincial Security alone.

This is the mode which without entering further into details I would venture humbly to suggest as the best, by which the assurances I was authorized to give that pecuniary relief would be proposed to Parliament may be fulfilled. It may indeed be contended there, that the Guarantee of a Colonial Debt is impolitic.

Upon this point however, Your Lordship, & H.M. Ministers will of course be prepared with a ready answer; but I may be permitted to remark, that if I know anything of the feelings of the British Population of Canada, the generosity of the Mother Country, will bind them to it more than ever, and if the opportunity I have now had of studying this Country has not been wholly thrown away, I am convinced that it is by such assistance, leading to so great practical results in the increase of the wealth and commerce of the Province, and of the comforts of its inhabitants that Great Britain may make the Colony less of a Burthen and far more a benefit to her, than it has ever before been.

I have &c.

(Signed)   SYDENHAM

CHAPTER V

THE act "to reunite the provinces of Upper and Lower Canada" received the assent of the Queen July 23, 1840, and the union was officially proclaimed on February 10, 1841. The winter was a busy one for Lord Sydenham. The Special Council of Lower Canada was spurred on to pass a series of most important acts; preparations had to be made for the coming elections and for the establishment of the new government. The relations with the United States caused some anxiety and the governor proved an implacable enemy.

Gov. House Montreal 24*th Feby* 1841

PRIVATE

My dear Lord John

No news of the 4th Feby Steamer so that I have nothing fresh from you nor any English accounts since the 6th Jany. My messenger must go tomorrow morning in spite of this or he may lose the Boat—Feby having but

28 days. It is a bore for I had hoped to have heard of your opening Parlt.

I have proclaimed my Union—summoned my Parlt.—issued my writs, and am up to my chin in work to get my offices properly distributed. This last no easy task, especially as the people must be secured before their Elections, almost all the principal people standing for some place or other, and most having to go three or four hundred miles to get returned—no joke in this country. The Elections will take place on the 8th, 15th, & 22d. March. In Upper Canada they must be over in 6 days, but in this province they may last till the day for the return of the writ. In Upper Canada they will be excellent. It is worthy of remark as indicating at least the spirit of the people towards me, that there is not one single Candidate who has not put out in his address that his object is to support my administration, on that point the harmony is wonderful. Of course they don't all mean what they say, but it shows at least that the expression of that intention is considered even by the Ultras on both sides as likely to do them good with the People. In Lower Canda, except in the Townships and perhaps one or two counties where the English prevail, we shall not have a man returned who does not hate British connexion, British rule, British improvements, and everything which has a taint of British feeling. The Electors themselves have no political opinions & do not generally, I believe, share in this feeling, but they are altogether in the hands of a little clique of Lawyers and Doctors who tell them all kinds of lies which it is impossible to contradict, as they can none of them read, and distrust the Seigneurs as much or more than they would do the British. However

I will produce a change in all this by the institutions I have given them and tho' the Assembly will at first probably be difficult to manage, I am quite satisfied that I *shall* be able to manage some of these fellows and beat the rest when they get returned and mixed up at Kingston with the Upper Canadians.

I have written you a Confidential dispatch upon the state of things, for though I had much rather tell you all my views in a private letter, yet in your ticklish condition it may be as well that something of that kind should appear officially in the Col. Office—but of course you will take care that my views of parties &c do not see the light of Parliament.[131]

I have had great difficulty in framing a list of names for the Legislative Council as regards the part to be selected for Lower Canada. Probably out of the 16 or 17 I send you 5 or 6 will either decline or be inadmissable for some reason. I wish there were more and better French names amongst them, but few are loyal, and of those some do not like the expense or trouble. Of the Upper Canada names, all will I have no doubt accept except one or two who may get into the Assembly or be unable to promise to attend on account of their private affairs and there is not one of them whom I do not personally know very well. Altogether, the solution is the best I could make and tolerably good. Qut of the 29 or 30 names I have sent[132] I shall without doubt be able to get 22 or 23 which will fulfil the provision of the act, and I can then add others as required without difficulty, or making the Council too large. It will be well if you can send me the Mandamuse's (sic) without in any formal document registering the names until you hear to whom

I have delivered them, as it might prove inconvenient that it should be noised about that Mr. So. & So had been accepted & then rejected by me. I have put Moffatt in after all. If possible let me have the Signs Manual by the Steamer of the 19th March.

I shall reduce the limits of Montreal & Quebec to the Cities & cut off the suburbs, which will cause a great clatter with the French and their Allies, but you might just as well have given no representation at all to either city as far as the Trade and the British Mercantile Interest is concerned, as not do so. *With* the suburbs, these Towns are as much French Counties as the Counties of the same names. The outcry will principally be raised at my reducing so much the constituencies to whom the choice of *two* members is confided. If I am attacked, I rely on you to defend me however, and Ellice may take the opportunity I should think also, for the alteration from one to two members was his, and the suggestion to reduce the limits to the suburbs for the purpose of securing mercantile representatives *his* too.

I had some difficulty in making my Special Council finish their business by the 10*th*. However like your Parliament as soon as I had fixed the day for their interment positively, they worked hard. I have got a very good Municipal Bill and Registry Law and to the working of these two measures I look for getting the Lower Canada population into better order. I was obliged to postpone the Judicature ordinances still further, for Stuart had made such a hash of them that I would not take on myself the responsibility of bringing them into operation without a Legislature to correct any blunders which might be discovered just at the moment of putting them

in force and when the old system would be at an end,
so I prolonged the time during which the Governor is
empowered to call the new system into operation till
December, which will give the United Parliament the
opportunity of correcting anything which may be faulty
in the details. You will perhaps see in the newspapers
that Stuart & I had a bruze. It is his misfortune that his
temper prevents his co-operating with anyone, and he
quarreled at last so decidedly with every member of the
Special Council, Lawyers and Laymen, that he compelled
me to let him go. However, as in spite of his temper to
others and the trouble that gives me I like him very much
and highly respect his talents. I would not let him be
run down, and we remained excellent friends to the great
annoyance of the world generally, I am afraid.

I thought it best to ask Sir George Arthur to stay on
for three weeks or a month after the proclamation of the
Union just to look to matters at Toronto, as all the
Govt. officers must go to their elections and I am obliged
to him for having consented. He will leave about the
middle of March, tho' I believe he is now getting rather
alarmed about going thro' the States, lest the Sovereign
People should shut him up like McCleod[133] (sic).

You will see by my dispatches the turn *that* has taken.
I trust that Fox will hear from Palmerston by the packet
of the 4th upon the first part of the question; if not, he
will bring this fresh outrage before the American Govt.
without waiting. Was there ever such a state of society in
a country pretending to be civilized? The Judges of the
land getting out of bed to render an account of their
conduct on the Bench to a committee chosen by the
Mob in the Street! and *not* an effort made by the civil

power to maintain order. It quite justifies Madame Roland's last saying. Unless we settle this whole question now with the American Government, we shall have nothing but trouble all along the frontier for the Yankees will take to arresting people as a good speculation; and there never was a better opportunity for compelling a settlement. The Americans are utterly unprepared for war and *cannot* engage in it, whilst we never were so well prepared on this side, which they know full well. I trust therefore that Palmerston will insist on reparation being made, and on a distinct understanding being arrived at that when the two Governments negotiate, the matter is to be settled by them, and not the separate States with whom we cannot deal.

Ever my dear Lord John
Yours very sincerely,
SYDENHAM

The financial situation was further explained in the following confidential despatch.

[*Copy*]

GOVERNMENT HOUSE MONTREAL 25 *Feby* 1841

CONFIDENTIAL

MY LORD,

By the messenger who arrived this morng. I have had the honor of receiving your Lordship's despatch No. 282, of the 11 January.

On the 22d Instant I anticipated your Lordship's wishes as conveyed to me in this Despatch by explaining the manner in which I venture to think that H.M. Govt. could best afford the assistance to the finances of this Province, which I was authorized to hold out on expectation of their receiving. I can add but little to what I had then the honor to submit, but I avail myself of the return of the Messenger to make one or two Remarks in consequence of what I find in your Lordship's letter to the Lords of the Treasury.

The plan which I have submitted implies the guarantee of a Loan to the extent of £1,500,000 which exceeds by a Sum of between 2 & 300,000£ the total debt of the Province. I took this amount because it was that to which I was authorized to go by the communication to which your Lordship refers, but I should not have done so if I was not satisfied that it is most desirable upon other grounds that the assistance to be rendered by the Imperial Govt. should not be limited to simply effecting a reduction in the Annual Charge for the Interest of the debt of Canada but that it is expedient in the interest both of the Province and of the Mother Country (if the latter interfere at all) to go beyond this.

I have already explained that the Debt of this Province having been contracted nearly altogether for public Works, which are now incomplete, & consequently unproductive, is in fact either a deadweight upon the Revenue of the Country, or a profitable investment of Capital, exactly according to the means which may be at the command of the Provincial Government. If no means can be found to finish these works either by an advance of money or by so improving the credit of the Province as to enable it to borrow in the Market at a rate of Interest not exorbitantly high, they must go to ruin, remain unproductive of any Revenue & in that case the Annual Charge for Interest is as much a dead weight upon the income of the Country as the Interest of the National Debt in England, the Capital of which has been expended in Armaments. The interference of Parlt. by affording its guarantee for this Debt would, under this supposition, do no more than reduce the Annual Charge upon the Provincial Revenue. The Capital already invested could not be rendered productive, and altho' the Province would undoubtedly be a gainer by the saving of interest, the advantage to it would stop there, whilst the security to the Mother Country for the repayment of Interest and Principal would be limited to the Ordinary Resources of the Colony, unaided by any return from the Work, for which the original Debt had been contracted.

On the other hand, however, if means are found thro' the assistance of Parlt. not only to effect the saving of the Interest on the debt already contracted, but to aid in rendering productive the works on which the Capital which they represent has been expended, the annual charge on the Provincial Funds is rendered light, & perhaps may be altogether removed, & the security to the Imperial Treasury in the same Ratio is improved and repayment rendered certain.

It is with this view that I do strongly recommend Parliament to go in its guarantee to the extent of the sum I have named, by which the double purpose will be served, & its own security stand in a far better position than it would otherwise do.

I would further remark with reference to an expression in your Lordship's letter to the Treasury, that my earnest hope is that whatever arrangement is affected with the consent of Parlt. will be made in England. Here we are in no condition to effect a transaction of this magnitude, or of this nature. The plan which I have had the honour of submitting is based upon this conviction—Let Parliament decide upon the terms on which it would consent to afford its guarantee for a fixed Sum—let it fix the conditions on which the present creditors of the Province shall receive back their Capital, or take fresh Stock under the Imperial Guarantee—let it declare the stipulations under which it will permit the surplus of the Loan which remains after the liquidation of the debt to be appropriated in the Province, that is for Public Works, solely under the responsibility of the Executive—let it affix the conditions which it deems advisable for its own security as to the Mortgage of the Provincial Revenues & of the Tolls—& let this arrangement—thus defined & regulated, be offered for the acceptance of the Provincial Legislature.

For this I have provided in the plan which I had the honor to submit.

There only remains one point on which it occurs to me that it may be desirable to add any thing. In the plan which I have given, the main principle consists in the compulsory repayment of their Capital to the Stockholders, notwithstanding the engagement entered upon with them that repayments should not be made for 15 or 16 years. On this it may be asserted that it is a violation of their Contract and therefore unjust to these parties.

That it breaks thro' the Contract is of course undeniable, but it is as impossible to deny that the arrangement, compulsory as it is, affords the most unexpected advantages to them, & if it were possible, as it is not, to propose it for their acceptance or refusal is such as not one of them would reject.

There is no other mode by which Parliament could afford its assistance with advantage to the Province or justice to itself, & the Creditors of Canada must be content if this course should not be adopted with the security they have at present. Hitherto, by continued loans & with infinite difficulty the interest upon the U. Canada Debt has been paid; but in spite of this, what is the Marketable value of these securities at the present time? If saleable at all the 5 perCent Stock may be worth 75 or 80, the 6 perCt. 85 or 90. For the moderate loan, required in this Province, where to the Security of the Revenue is superadded that of the Tolls on the Canal or the Turnpike Road for which the money is required, I am even now daily compelled to authorize the payment of an Interest of 7 & 7½ perCent. The Montreal Harbour Bonds, the best security in America, because the actual Tolls receivable must inevitably pay both Capital & Interest,—sell at this moment at 90 perCent Debentures. It seems to me then perfectly idle to suppose that more than a full measure of Justice will not be given to the creditors of the Province under the arrangement I have suggested. Not one can receive less than he advanced for the stock has never been above par at or under which it was taken, whilst at present no one can obtain within 15 or 20 perCent of that amount for it, or if this arrangement be not effected ever probably hope to get more.

Your Lordship will I hope forgive my entering so much at length into these details, but the extreme anxiety which I feel to be furnished with the decision of Her Majesty's Government before the opening of the Legislature, and the conviction to which I have arrived after the best consideration that no other plan is possible, must plead my excuse.

I have etc.

(Signed) SYDENHAM

MONTREAL 10*th April* 1841

PRIVATE

MY DEAR LORD JOHN

I have fortunately very little to say to you for I cannot write and am not very fit to dictate. The doctors thought me gone last Monday but I got thro' it I suppose to show them that they know nothing about either killing or curing. I shall be weak I am afraid for some time, and as they have coaxed the gout into the hands and will do nothing to give it a chance of jumping again to the stomach or heart it may be some time before I can hold a pen.

Your despatch by the B. Queen arrived yesterday but we have not got the mail by Cunard of the 19th. I thought that McLeod's affair would create a great feeling in England, for so it ought, but I did not believe that that ridiculous report of the Committee on Foreign Relations of the Assembly would have raised such a clatter. In England you are perhaps not aware that the Assembly on such subjects carries very little weight with it: in fact nothing can be lower than that Body, and it is not in the slightest degree like the House of Commons in England either in character, attributes, or power. The men who go there are generally lawyers and people of not much weight who find the allowance convenient and can generally follow some practice of business at Washington. The Senate and the local Senates and Assemblies absorb the greater part of the talent that is to be found in the States. But this clatter will do no harm but good—the Americans are only to be frightened into proper terms, and their press which was excessively alarmed at first had begun to shake its feathers again and say that two mails had arrived from England and that all excitement had subsided.

I now wait with great anxiety to hear what you determine about McLeod. Palmerston's note though strong only renews the demand for his release and warns the Govt. of the danger of refusing, but something more must now be done. McLeod is incarcerated for several months and doubtless the object of the American Govt. will be to exchange notes and prolong the negotiations until his trial can take place when they would probably succeed in liberating him, and thus evade the question. This I trust you will not permit but I much doubt whether anything short of an order to Fox to quit Washington if your demand be not at once complied with will prevent it, and this therefore I hope may at once be done.

I will keep the people quiet here and I fear no outbreak on the frontier, but this can only be done by putting a stop to the Lynch law on the American side.

I am afraid that there will be a new difficulty in the States but it is an additional ground of weakness to them— the last accounts I had despaired of old Tippecanoe's life,[134] if he goes the vice-president succeeds for the whole term Mr. Tyler. I can learn little about him but he is not supposed to be well with either Clay or Webster—he is a Virginian selected as they always are in the States from the South when the President happens to be from the North.

They have made a great piece of work in the American papers and in some of the rabid journals of this Province about the violence at our elections. Sir George Arthur will tell you how quietly everything passed off in the Upper Province, with the exception of that unfortunate

disturbance at Toronto which however was after the
election, and here considering that two years ago the
people were cutting each other's throats and in arms
against each other whilst the French Canadian press
and leaders have been doing everything in their power
to excite the passions of the People, I am quite surprised
that they went off so well. That scoundrel Mr. Lafontaine,
who after arming his people with dirks and bludgeons
loaded with lead was scared away by a few Irishmen,
has tried to divert the attention of his friends who were
furious with him by writing an address abusing me and
pretending to retail a conversation with me last Feby
twelve-month in which he says I wanted to buy him. I
need not say the whole is a lie from beginning to end, and
it is felt to be so because his friends know that he would
have jumped at any price. He is a cantankerous fellow
without talent & not worth buying or I would have had
him when I pleased.

Pray let me have the Mandamuses for the counsellors
(sic) whose names I have sent, *without fail* by the steamboat
of the 4th for I may find myself puzzled to complete the
number for Lower Canada. By that steamer they will
reach me before the opening of Parlt. on the 26th.

I got yesterday a paper with a report of Philpott's
speech[135] on the Seminary ordinance.[136] I wish I was
strong enough to send you a dispatch on one or two
points. What a shocking liar! for I am satisfied that he
must have invented the greater part of his facts and well
[A portion of this letter is missing.]

If the ordinance is rejected, about which personally
however I care not a straw as it is no legislation of mine,
the House of Lords will have alienated the only Body of

Catholic Clergy in the Province who are firm in the support of the British Crown and it will be indeed nuts to the country clergy and the agitators.

Ever etc.
(Signed) SYDENHAM

GOVT. HOUSE MONTREAL 12th April 1841

PRIVATE

MY DEAR LORD JOHN

I received yesterday your two letters of the 18th March by the Acadia after my despatches had been sent off for her, but I start a messenger in hopes of still reaching Boston before she sail in order to take you an amended list of Legislative Counsellors (sic), if there should be anything in the doubt raised about the single instrument.

I do not know what your lawyers may decide; the expression is certainly strong, "an instrument," but Sir Alured Clarke,[137] who acted upon the same words, issued separate writs of summons [for the legislative council of Lower Canada, 1792] which were the only ones registered here, and I suppose what he did was legal. Whether he did so on a single or many signs Manual I cannot find out. I rather think the first, but either would form a precedent for what I have to do in case I do not get the amended return in time to use it; so I shall not be very uneasy about it. Your answer if sent to me by the 4th will certainly reach me by the 26th May so it is not worth while to have a fresh prorogation for this purpose.[138]

I should be far more inclined to defer the meeting on another ground, namely, your *guarantee* that it would be necessary to do so for fifteen days in order to be of any service,—and that would be too long. If your Budget really comes on the 30th April I can however hear the result of your proposal by that same boat of the 4th, and it is all important that I should have the power of stating something about it in my speech. Still I know too well by experience what fixing days for Budgets means to feel sure of its being actually produced on the 30th, so I shall be infinitely obliged to you if you will tell me privately how far I may go upon the subject with my Parliament; if no more ever can be permitted than a general expression of a desire on the part of the Government to propose measures to the Imperial Parlt. to assist in settling the financial affairs of Canada, it will be better than nothing. Pray let me have what I may say in this way if accident should prevent your enabling me to be more explicit. I shall want all you can do, for people will be grievously angry about the Timber duties and I shall have an up hill battle to fight about that. However, I shall not shrink from that, and do not want to get rid of my share of the responsibility of the change even though I am Governor-General of B.N. America. But you must of course give us time, and not think of making the alterations of the duty applicable to the shipments this year, which would be grossly unfair and indeed was expressly provided against in the report of my committee of 1835. I should say indeed from what I have seen here that by far your wisest course as well as the fairest to Colonial interests would be to do as *at last* in 1831—diminish the difference between Baltic & Colonial by three or four steps. Raising the duty on Colonial timber will be popular here rather than taking it the other way.[139]

I shall not hesitate to detain the Regiments relieved if

I think there is any danger, but I apprehend little chance of an actual war at present, though if you are not firm about MacCleod (sic) you may have one some time hence when you are less well prepared for it and the Americans better. I feel quite confident that if you lose the present opportunity of bringing these matters to a test by insisting on McLeod's liberation conte qui conte you will repent it, and, I would much rather have seen a demand to that effect in Palmerston's note which you send me, than what I find there which seems to me rather to weaken than to strengthen the previous one, and I say this because I feel sure that it would not disturb the peace at present, whilst it would also ensure it for the future.

No man can say how the feelings of so mobile a people as the Americans may be upon any point six months from the time he speaks,—but at present I am satisfied they dread war with England. They are too a calculating people, and fight not for glory but to plunder, which they know they cannot now get in Canada. You must not in the least heed their speeches and declarations in their popular assemblies. They are such a set of braggadocios and there is such a submission on the part of their public men to pander to this vanity and self sufficiency, that their language is always in the superlative but their acts are very different. Mr. Pickens, in explaining that his report was a peaceable one, blurted out the whole character and conduct of his countrymen when he said that he did not mean war,[140]—all he wished was to frighten us by abuse and Billingsgate.

In two or three years I hope that we shall have a good hold over the vastly increasing population of the Western States by their interest thro' the St. Lawrence, indeed we have some now. The Eastern seaboard is certainly with us, and the South have their cotton interest as well as their slave fears, so that I really anticipate no cause for alarm of war being rashly entered upon thro' the ambition or restlessness of the people, if we can once put an end to these Border feuds which have now endangered the peace and which will inevitably do so again unless brought to a head.[141]

I am delighted with Philpott's thorough defeat. Pray thank Normanby for his speech from me as I cannot write, but after all it is amusing enough that Nicolet, the point on which it seems it all turned with you, is really no precedent at all. However the noble Lord who did not know that the Roman Catholic Religion was an established religion in Canada may be excused for not understanding the difference between a lay and ecclesiastical corporation.[142]

I am gaining strength as you may judge from my having dictated this long letter. I got out of bed yesterday for the first time.

Ever, my dear Lord John
Your's most truly
SYDENHAM

GOV. HOUSE MONTREAL 26th April 1841

PRIVATE

MY DEAR LORD JOHN

I am a great deal better but I still cannot write with my right hand.

I have your's of the 3rd April and your dispatches by the Caledonia.

So your lawyers have decided that the summons for the

Legislative Counsellors (sic) must be in one instrument, and seem to make it apply to my summons as well as to the Sign Manual. This may be law, but the latter part of it is certainly not practice, and if they are correct the Legislative Council from 1791 to 1837 was an illegal Body, because as I have before told you it was constituted by Sir Alured Clarke under separate writs. So much for lawyers interpretations and Govt. practice! but it does not much signify for I am now sure to receive the amended list before Parlt. meets, as I shall have to defer it from the 26th May to the 9th or 10th June. The season is so late, the navigation not being yet open, that I am compelled to do this, partly on account of the difficulty of communication, and partly from the seed time being thrown so far back that the attendance of members before the abovementioned day could not be obtained. I am sorry to have been obliged to submit to this postponement but I cannot help myself, & at all events it will secure the matter of the Council and will give me besides the chance of another mail, that of the 19th May, bringing me a final account of my money matters from you.

I shall keep the separate writs however until I get the list and then return you those which are not wanted.

I never read such a vague and unmeaning document as that you send me from the three Companies[143] about pecuniary assistance to be afforded by them for improvements in Canada, indeed if it were not for your dispatch which accompanies it, it would be perfectly unintelligible. Even with that however I cannot make out what they propose to do, and I must tell you this officially next mail. My own opinion is that this proposal or rather hint, for there is no definite proposal, is nothing more than a puff to the Public, and a blind to the Shareholders. One company is bankrupt—another has not raised its capital at all, & can't pay for the estate it has purchased—and the third, the Canada, has all its funds employed already. Still if anything is to be got out of them I am quite ready to jump at it, if they will only condescend to particulars; I shall be very glad therefore if you will close at once with their proposal to send out an agent who can explain what they really mean and treat with me here, and he should come directly that he may find us in session when, if the business is to be done, it may be arranged. But don't let me have Wakefield whom I have heard talked of,[144] we have scamps enough already in the Province without him.

You will see by a dispatch I send you that there is a mess about the disallowance of the two naturalization ordinances.[145] I care nothing about them except for the credit of the Govt which should be consistent, and not declare a thing to be illegal in 1841 which it found perfectly legal in 1840. The opinion from the B. of Trade too is a manifest blunder.

I have nothing fresh about McLeod's affair, but the American lawyers are making out a great case justifying the burning of the Caroline, and in the meantime McLeod remains in gaol and unless you interfere will be there for months.

Harvey has been trying to get white-washed by the Legislature of N. Brunswick for his conduct on the Boundary question which I think is very bad taste as well as very impudent. If he had confined their vote of approval and remuneration of 1500£ to his services as Civil Governor, it would have been very fair, but now he sets up the Legislature of N. Brunswick who can know

nothing of the matter against you and me by making
them lug in the Boundary question in their vote. I am
very glad that Colbroke[146] (sic) is come.

Eyer & e.

SYDENHAM

MONTREAL 25 *May* 1841

PRIVATE

MY DEAR LORD JOHN

I can at last write to you myself. I have had a
very distressing illness, but am recovering I hope pretty
fast, and have now not much pain to complain of; only
great debility. Grey will have told you the reason you did
not hear from me last mail. I shall move up to Kingston
tomorrow, as I can perform the journey nearly all the
way by water and without much fatigue. I was very lucky
that I deferred the meeting of my Parlt. till the 14th
June, as I could not have got there by the 26th, the day I
first settled. Now, I am pretty sure to be at Kingston at
least, and I will go down to the House if I am carried
there in a litter. I *think* that I shall do well with them,
but the first month will probably be a little stormy. The
Upper Canadian Radl. will be inclined to join the
French in opposition to the Civil List and some other
crotchets, but when I get well amongst them I have great
hopes of keeping things right with the Members by the
personal influence I have with the Upper Canadians.
Your squeamishness about the repayment of the Canada
Bond holders greatly increases my difficulty however [147]
With a vote of the House of Commons I could have
opened brilliantly; now, I shall have nothing but promises
to give them and it is difficult to make any arrangement

by which the said Bond holders will not come in for the Lion's share of the benefit of Imperial guarantee, to the detriment of course of the Province. But I will do my best. The first list of Mandamus's for the Legislative Council will also, I hope, be here before the 14th and I shall be relieved from that difficulty. 20 out of the 24 proposed members have accepted so that I can comply with the act according to *your* Lawyer's reading of it, if I get the new list in time.

You will learn the result of McLeod's affair most probably by this packet tho' I do not yet know of it here, the judges having taken time to consider. There is little doubt I am informed of its' being in favor of his liberation—but that does not settle the question and Capt. D.[148] or any other English man will be liable to be seized and imprisoned for six months just as McCleod (sic) has been, if they can lay hold of him in the States. I must say that I agree with Fox in thinking that you might have acted with more energy in this matter. In spite of all their fair words the Americans have fenced with us at last. The Govr. of the State of New York, a sworn friend of the present administration, has taken care to declare that the Central Govt. did *not* interfere in the matter, and the latter kept away their Attorney General & made a public declaration that the motion for Habeas Corpus was made solely on the responsibility of the accused & his Counsel. By the bye who is to pay the expenses of these proceedings, I have advanced money, because I could not allow McCleod (sic) to be hanged for want of Counsel, but it comes from the Military Chest of course & cannot be made a charge upon the Province. I don't think that you sufficiently understand the character of Jonathan. He will never be fair or just unless he is compelled, but he will always yield if you are firm. The only advantage, which is one of words indeed, which Fox or Palmerston have given him in the discussion of the Caroline is the one of the word "Piratical" and upon that you see Webster writes a volume, and gives some hard hits: I cannot understand why that expression was ever used, for I agree with Webster, the Americans were not *Pirates* in the Caroline affair.

You have taken a pretty bold step,[149] and I am all impatience to learn the result which must of course have been arrived at by this time—but whatever it be, I sincerely rejoice at your having taken your stand with the Country upon a great & intelligible, and above all a practical measure of Reform. It has everything to recommend it in what it touches and in what it lets alone. It does *not* meddle with Religious prejudices; it does *not* relate to Ireland. It does *not* touch any of the theoretical questions of Govt. on which parties have so long been divided. It *is* a new Flag to fight under and must prevail eventually, whatever be its' success now. The only criticism·I should be disposed to pass on your proceeding is the mode of introducing the question. I think you might have made a greater effect if you had disconnected it from the Budget, but at a distance it is not easy to judge of tactics and that might have been impossible. I conclude however that you will have determined on dissolution, if Peel goes against you which of course with the class interests on your side, must be fatal to the measure—and even then you will probably be beaten—but you will at least have got a Parlt. returned upon your own ground of battle, and be able hereafter either to compel the Tories to adopt the measure themselves, or when they split amongst themselves, which in power is inevitable, be in a good condition to go back.

I cannot say either that I altogether approve of the mode in which you propose to carry out your principle with regard to Timber.[150] Raising the duty to 20s is in fact at variance with it, and as Revenue for *this* year, it must fail; for you will be beaten out of the imposition of this new duty on the present importations, I feel sure. The People here have taken the matter much more philosophically than was to be expected, but at Quebec where the Lumber Merchants reside, they are at boiling point.

So Wakefield has arrived after all. I have not yet been able to see him, but I am told that he is determined to support my Govt.—it cannot be for long tho' as I can do nothing for that horrible swindle of Beauharnois[151] even if I were ever so much inclined. However I shall try to keep him out of mischief at all events.

Believe me my dear Lord John

Your's ever most truly

SYDENHAM

P.S.—I have sent you a dispatch which will enable you to deal with my R.C. Bishop when he applies to you. I made it "secret" because I do not know whether Philpotts might not hang us both if he got hold of it.

KINGSTON 12*th June*, 1841

PRIVATE

MY DEAR LORD JOHN,

I have your letter of the 18th May by the Halifax Boat. I scarcely can guess whether this will find you still at the Colonial Office, but I heartily trust that it will. You will of course have been beaten on Sugar—but I hope that you will then have given them Timber and then Corn, the discussions could only do you great good, and the enemy no less mischief. Defeated you would certainly be, but unless money matters prevented it, which I suppose Baring would take care to provide—you could then dissolve with effect, and either obtain a majority, or if as I fear, there was no chance of that against the combined efforts of the Clods and the Class interests, get together a Parliament elected upon new principles and one in which your minority would eventually prevail. I have read your speech upon opening the debate on the Sugar question with feelings of admiration and pleasure which I cannot describe. The Free Traders have never been orators since Mr. Pitt in early days.—We hammered away with facts and figures and some argument, but we could not elevate the subject and excite the feelings of the People. At last, you who can do both have fairly under-taken it, and the cause has a Champion worthy of it. I regret that I am not once more on the Treasury Bench to enjoy the triumph and lend my small assistance in the fight, but you do not want it, and it is most gratifying to me to hear from you that I have been of some service to you here at least.

I am in the thick of preparation for the session which opens the day after to-morrow and promises, I am sorry to say, to be a very stormy one. I have got my "*crisis*" too. Baldwin, the Sols. Genl., who is the most crotchety impracticable enthusiast I ever had to deal with has decided upon joining the Rump of the old Lower Can-adian assembly whom he designates as Reformers and

I expect his resignation to-day, or else that I shall be
obliged myself to turn him out. But I have a case against
him which will I am confident destroy him, and I do not
believe that he can carry with him more than five or
six of the Upper Canada members, which with the
French party may give 25 or 30 opposition. But we shall
have motions on responsible Govt., want of confidence,
the details of the Union, and everything that is most
mischievous because their agitation will destroy all
confidence in Canadian tranquility & Canadian credit
in England, however successful I may be in defeating
them. Wakefield, who is here for his Companie (sic) and
who has been promising millions to those People if they
will be quiet and not make fools of themselves, sparing
I must do him the justice to say no efforts to convince
them of the ruin to themselves and the misery to the
Province which their conduct must bring on, is in despair
and thinks the game up. *I* do not and I feel confident
that I can lick this Ultra-party completely, altho' I
certainly cannot prevent the mischief which the agitation
they will cause will do to the prospects of the Province.
Nous verrons—I am alas too weak and suffering still to
be quite up to the business, but I shall do my best.

By the bye I could not write to you privately last mail
about Baldwin's absurd refusal to take the oath of
Supremacy but I beg you will send me the opinion of
the Law Officers whether he can be excused from it
under the Commission I hold. My own opinion is that he
cannot, and that I ought not to have allowed him to
dispense with it—yet as it had been done in Upper
Canada when he took office under Sir Francis Head, I
did not like to persist in my refusal as I believe I ought

to have done. His own opinion on the point of law which I have sent you seems to me the veriest nonsense, and Day's not much better.[152] Unfortunately, both Attorneys General were absent from Montreal and I could not get theirs, but I now hear that they both think that the oath could not be dispensed with under the terms of the Commission. Pray let me have a decision on the point. I shall be very glad if my *act* is wrong and my *opinion* right. As the last steamer from Halifax was delayed ten days you will get this letter and the dispatch nearly at the same time.

I am greatly embarrassed by your squeamishness about the Public faith to the Canadian Creditor, because without the compulsory repayment I do not know how I can prevent his reaping all the advantage of the guarantee which you agree to give, and thus depriving the Province of it. However I shall endeavor to concoct a measure and send it home.[153] I shall give the substance of your dispatch upon Finance, Emigration, & Defence in my Speech and then give the Assembly extracts from it as far as I prudently can.

I think we shall do very well at Kingston. I have really a very fair house for the Assembly and Council to meet in and the accommodation would be thought magnificent by us Members of the English House of Commons. But the fellows in these Colonies have been spoiled by all sorts of luxuries, large arm chairs, desks with stationery before each man, & heaven knows what, so I suppose they will complain. The House I lodge in is really a very nice one, or rather will be when finished, which will just fit the arrival of my Successor, and the Public Offices are far better than either at Montreal or Toronto—but the confusion of the move is tremendous, and the practical consumation of the Union is I assure you far from a honey moon.[154]

You must be looking out for a successor to me, if you are still in, very shortly, as I hope that nothing will prevent my leaving business in August or the early days of Septr. Indeed my medical men tell me that if I would ever so much, I must not stay much later than that. The only name who occurs to me as being really thoroughly qualified to do justice to this Govt. (if good can indeed be done) is George Grey. Some time ago, I know that he was anxious to go to one of the Presidencies in India. Would he take it? his position must be rather a disagreeable one with Howick's antics. If he would come, I really think that in the interest of the Colony and your own, should you remain, he is the fittest person by far that could be found, and I would strongly recommend you, if there was a probability that the Tories might succeed in ousting you shortly, to a point &.send him out even earlier than you would otherwise do, in order to secure his coming. I would stay with *him* for a fortnight or three weeks if he wished in order to give him all the information and assistance I could to start him.

I am all anxiety to hear of your next move.

Ever, my dear Lord John,
Yours most sincerely,
SYDENHAM

P.S.—Wakefield has written a long letter to Buller upon the state of things here which he sent to *me open to read.* As I know that Buller is very communicative of his letters he may perhaps shew it to you. It is full of blunders upon some matters owing to his want of correct information, especially in his idea that the 15 or 20 Lower Canadian Rebels could be bought to support any Govt. however constituted. Unless Buller himself shews you the letter, do not mention it, or ask for it however.

KINGSTON 27 *June* 1841

PRIVATE

MY DEAR LORD JOHN

I gave you rather a melancholy account of my position & prospects by the last packet. Tho' I was satisfied that I could not be mistaken in my opinion of the Parliament, I felt uneasy at the course which matters were taking, and was not so sure that it might not take *time* to get things right, which it was important with regard to the effect to be produced on public opinion in England on Canadian matters, to avoid. A stormy opening would have damaged our credit there almost irretrievably, because People only look to the great features of the case, and will not take the trouble or give the time to understand the details. So I felt nervous at my crisis.

I have gained the most complete victory. I have got rid of Baldwin and finished him as a public man for ever.[155] I have done so without his being able to carry away with him one single supporter of mine. The only two Upper Canada members he can get to vote with him being noted agitators of little weight whose return I could prevent to-morrow if they went to their constituents. I have left him leading the rump of the old Lower Canada Assembly, a party of 12 or 14 only, for the other Canadian members altho' they have gone with him in opposing the Union, which he has had the baseness to do after all that has passed, will leave him on other questions. I have got my House into capital order—a sure majority of two to one upon any question I chuse and in support of my administration; and whoever follows me may now, with management, keep everything quiet and rule with comfort. There may be a little bickering about the Civil List but I do not dread it. All the topics that could be brought forward to test the House came on in the debate on the Address which lasted according to the practice of this country three or four days. Baldwin's resignation— Confidence in the administration—responsible Govt.— the Parliamentary terms of the Union—on all we came off triumphant in debate, and divisions, and I have the House completely in hand. I can give you no better proof than one occurrence. They introduced some rather ambiguous words about the Union, and passed them in Committee in spite of my Cabinet. I sent for the Members who I knew had voted only from ignorance, not intention, and away they went directly and voted the words out again upon the report, by a very large majority!

It has been no easy matter to do all this for I have it all on my own shoulders. My Lower Canadian members of the Govt. know none of the people of the Upper Province and those from Upper Canada are unluckily unpopular. Harrison, the Civil Secretary,[156] the best man I have, is unluckily not in the House, tho' he will be returned by acclamation next week for Kingston. Then, they have none of them the slightest notion of carrying on a Govt. in the House, so I am obliged to be *Leader* myself which as I cannot go there is awkward, & takes up a great deal of time. What between lecturing Members every morning & schooling my Cabinet every day my hands are therefore pretty full. However, I have certainly as good men in the Govt. as are to be found and when they learn the new system and acquire confidence, I have no doubt they will do very well. And, which is the principal point, I have three fourths of the Assembly with *me* personally, and a perfect certainty, felt not only by myself, but by *them* that if they were to pretend to oppose me, their Constituents would send them to the right about on the first opportunity. So you may consider the problem to be solved and my work done. The session will be a quiet one and I shall carry the measures I want and have a well established system for those who succeed me.

What I have seen however, and had to do in the course of the last three weeks strengthens my opinion of the absolute necessity of your sending as my successor some one with House of Commons & ministerial habits—a person who will not shrink from work, & who will govern, as I do, *himself.* George Grey is the man, if you can get him to come.

I hope you will approve of my speech. It has produced great effect thro' all the Province and even brought over the grumblers of Quebec in spite of the Timber duties. The dispatch which I propose giving to the House is your's of the 3d May. I object to giving dispatches in general, unless I am ordered, but this is so important & so valuable, and above all so calculated to immortalize your Administration of the Colonies in Canada that I have decided on sending it to the Legislature. By the bye I have written a dispatch to you about a pretended quotation from me of Peel's.[157] Use it or not, as you think best. My object is, not to be Hansardized to such expres-

sions as he chuses to put into my mouth. I have thought
it best to record in a dispatch[158] also my opinion of the
present state of matters in Parlt. here and the dismissal
of Baldwin. My letter to him will appear to you rather
long, but he had a reputation, (a most undeserved one)
for honesty, and was besides the leader of a party. It was
necessary therefore to destroy the one, and cut off the
other, both of which I could not feel sure of doing without
a full account of the transaction.

I am all impatient for the result of Peel's want of
confidence motion, of which I have only the three first
day's (sic) report for I certainly did not expect that there
could have been any doubt, as it seems there still is, of
his carrying it. If he has failed, it is indeed a blunder!
But I conclude, succeed or fail, the dissolution will have
taken place by this time. I am delighted that you have
adopted the course you have—you will have seen that it
is exactly that which I hoped for. Gillespie tells me that
you are to be returned for the City. Of all your achieve-
ments I do not know so extraordinary a one as that you
should have made *him* wish for it, as I believe he really
does!

I wish that you would speak to Minto about removing
Capt. Sandom[159] from here. He is a most unfit person to
be in command, & after the issue of the Court Martial on
Capt. Dawes in which he so signally failed, and put the
country to enormous expence, he really ought not to be
allowed to remain in Canada even if his temper did not
wholly disqualify him for such a command. Pray get him
away quietly, if you can, which I should think was easy,
as his time has expired long ago. He is protected by
Adams and others at the Admiralty, but the mischief

which keeping him here does after all that has passed is very great.

Ever my dear Lord John[160]

Your's very sincerely

SYDENHAM

GOVT. HOUSE KINGSTON 12*th July* 1841

PRIVATE

MY DEAR LORD JOHN

I have your's of the 18 June. I have little to tell you about things here. They go better and better every day, for altho' my House Assembly has done very little real business yet, their *no* progress has been far from useless to *me*. My Govt. people are learning their business, and the opposition, such as it were, is dwindling down to the most contemptible affair possible. I have several measures introduced, and more ready. The delay has been caused by the absurd nature of the Upper Canada Law for the trial of Election Petitions. The old Granville act, calculated for a House of 600 members was transplanted bodily to Upper Canada, and so in a House of 84 members of whom one third are petitioned against they have been in a dead fix, as the Yankees call it, for a Ballot. A whole week has been lost in trying to get a quorum as fixed by law and the House has been obliged to adjourn day after day without doing anything. They actually came to me to ask me to prorogue them for a couple of days in order to get them out of the scrapes, but I laughed at them and told them that I would dissolve them if they liked and see what their constituents would say to them. So by sending all over the country we have to-day got a quorum for the Ballot, and now shall go to real business. You would laugh at the various parts I am called upon to play. One of them is to give them all the House of Commons precedents, in which I am become a greater authority than Hatsell! I am engaged just now however on a measure which I would rather carry and make perfect than anything I have ever done, because it will not only be of great benefit to the country, but will set an example to England of which I shall take advantage when I get back. It is the establishment of a perfectly sound paper Currency by one Government Bank of Issue to the entire exclusion of all other Paper payable on demand. The same scheme which I wanted to have adopted in 1833, but for which certainly the Public mind was not then prepared, and that which has been since so ably developed by Sam Lloyd, your Proposer in the City. There never was such an opportunity for the trial, or circumstances so favorable to it, for the charters of nearly all the Banks in the Province are expiring which puts them at my mercy, and I have not the least doubt from the absence of any decent currency in the United States that in two or three years such a Bank would obtain for its paper the circulation of all the bordering States, which would tax Jonathan for our benefit 80 or 100,000£ a year. My chief difficulty arises from there not being a man in either House who knows the a.b.c. of these questions and to whom therefore I could entrust my measure with any confidence—but I make the members all come to me and lecture them, so I am not without hopes of success. You will understand however that the rest goes on very fairly when I am willing to *volunteer* such a great plan.[161]

This and other measures will probably make the

session a long one tho', and therefore I shall send you by the next packet, as you desire, my formal resignation, that you may either send me a successor yourself or that the Tories may be certain to give me one, or at least let *me* get away in the middle of September whether they do so or not. I shall have prorogued Parliament, and have had a fortnight or three weeks to clear up matters afterwards, by that time I reckon! but it would not do for me to wait till I have actually done so, in order to *ask* for my [illeg.], as that would throw back my departure till the end of October or the beginning of November which is more than my health will allow.

I am afraid from all that I hear that I shall find you *out* indeed it is not to be expected that you can beat the Squires and the Class Interests together—but the course you have taken is, I am quite sure, the right one, and is certain to make the great cause in which you have embarked ultimately successful. I think you have done most wisely as well as nobly in consenting to stand for the City. The occasion demanded a great effort and you have done more than your part.

Believe me ever my dear Lord John
Your's most truly
SYDENHAM

GOVT. HOUSE KINGSTON 27*th July* 1841 [162]

PRIVATE

MY DEAR LORD JOHN

I have received your letter of the 3d July. You will have received shortly after a far different account of things here from that which you then had—you are right

however in saying that after all if matters had not turned
out as they have, all that our opposition could do under
the Union Act would be to retard the prosperity of the
Colony. But then I have a sort of Parent's pride in
promoting that and therefore altho' the Government
could have been conducted, and so far as England is
concerned I do not think you would have been troubled,
my hopes and projects would have been disappointed by
the delay, and I should not have felt satisfied that the
work I had carved out for myself was done, altho' what
you had given me to do was. So I am well pleased that
it has turned out otherwise. The People are very slow
and lose a great deal of time in useless chatter—they may
often carry very foolish motions too—and I may perhaps
not get all I want through—but I shall, even in this
session, carry many most important & useful measures
and the rest will follow. Even Wakefield, a grumbler by
trade, goes back perfectly satisfied that the Union is
firmly and irrevocably established, and the new Govt.
thoroughly organized in fact, that all that is essential is
complete, and that time will render the working of the
system more easy.

I am very much obliged to you for your promised leave
of absence as that will enable me to come away when the
Doctors order me without being at the mercy of your
Tory successors if unhappily you get one, and it neatly
answers what I desired. I send you however my formal
resignation, because nothing would tempt me to return
here under Stanley or Lord Aberdeen, and besides as I
am compelled on account of my health to be absent
during the winter at all events, I am not of opinion that
it would be right to leave the Province without a real

Governor for so long. So pray consider it as final and submit it to the Queen.

I am afraid that it will be one of your last acts in Downing St., for of course they will turn you out on the address or immediately afterwards, if they can ever keep their violent spirits in order about a speaker. What will Peel do? Even with the majority *you* give him and which is more than he believes himself (as I am told), he will find the Government next to impossible, for of course he must *discount* a certain number from his supporters whom disappointment will turn into Patriots. Between Ireland, a deficient Revenue and fresh taxes, the Poor Law on which so many of his own supporters are pledged, and a liberal minority of 310 or 15 he will have enough to do!

So you will see that the New York State Court[163] have decided in opposition to Webster as well as to law and common sense and McLeod remains in gaol. He will take his trial at the Assizes in September & I suppose be acquitted, for Jonathan will most likely be satisfied with having bullied us and not proceed to find him guilty & hang him; tho' even of that there is no certainty. It will depend on what the Sovereign mob hints to the Judge and the Jury or whether they are Loco focoes or Whigs. But what is to be the result? There are a vast number of people on the border who actually were at the burning of the "Caroline," and indeed Judge Cowan's doctrine extends to all who fought even in the American war. A Sympathizer has only to get hold of one of them and as he is to be punished in spite of his having acted under authority if he is really guilty of this new offence, he is sure of being hanged. It is altogether a sad mess, for it is now too late to insist on McLeod's return conte qui conte. The excitement has fortunately blown off here a good deal, & I have no difficulty in keeping the people quiet or from taking the law into their own hands.

I have had Mr. Howe here, the Nova Scotian ex-agitator whom I converted into an Executive Counsellor. He gives a most coleur de rose account of things there, and of the working of the system, which confirms Falkland's account to me and greatly pleases me. Howe is an excellent man when properly managed & controlled and has fully answered my expectations. I should be glad of him here.

Will you have the kindness to approve my office and money arrangements upon which I send you two dispatches by this mail as I do not wish to be at the mercy of either a new Colonial Secretary or of Fremantle or Granville Somerset at the Treasury?

Ever my dear Lord John

Your's most truly

SYDENHAM

Lest his friend should forget, Sydenham asked Lord John Russell to secure for him a further mark of royal approbation of his work.

KINGSTON 27th July 1841

CONFIDENTIAL

My DEAR LORD JOHN

You will have to lay my formal resignation of office before the Queen, & I believe that it is usual either on the acceptance of it, or upon the return home of the departing Functionary to confer some mark of favor if he has done his duty. I find that nearly all those who have held high civil rank in the Colonies or abroad, all indeed who have filled the same station that I have, have received the G.C.B.[164]—Auckland before going out to India—Sir Charles Metcalfe on returning—Gosford on his return after failure in Canada, & in addition to his English Peerage—Most of the Ministers or Ambassadors abroad. Probably therefore the Queen may be disposed to confer the same distinction on me upon my quitting this Country and returning home, and if so, I should hope that it would be upon *your* recommendation when H.M. accepts my resignation, so that I may find it done on my return, and not have to look for it or receive it at Tory hands.

Of course I shall be very glad of it in order to show that my administration of affairs has been satisfactory up to its' conclusion, & that I have not merely carried the Union, but have also worked out my own system, and governed these great Provinces to the end of my stay, advantageously to them and to the Crown.

I shall also feel great pleasure in getting it as an admission of "*Complete Success.*" You know perhaps that there was a question giving it me *before* I started from England, when Lord Melbourne recommended me not to press it as he said it might make the Peerage to which he was pledged less easy for him in the *event of my failing.* He wrote "nothing but the most decided and complete success could justify the giving both, and if it come at all doubtful as it may very easily be, not only without any fault of your's but consistently with the greatest merit it would become impossible to superadd the additional honor to that which would already have been conferred." The question therefore is raised whether I have completely succeeded or not, and it would be most gratifying to me to have it solved in the affirmative.

In your hands however I leave the matter, being perfectly satisfied that you will do what is most kind to me.

Ever My dear Lord John

Your's most truly

SYDENHAM

GOVT. HOUSE KINGSTON 4th Augt. 1841[165]

PRIVATE

MY DEAR LORD JOHN

As according to my calculation, which I fear may be too true, this will probably be the last opportunity by which you will hear from me as Secretary of State, (until the next turnout) I send you a short public dispatch[166] upon our proceedings here, and I am sure you will learn with pleasure that they go on so prosperously. I have got thro' three most important measures already and if the session produced no more we should have done good service—but the rest will follow rapidly, and I do not despair even of carrying my Bank Scheme which is quite an *Extra*. Of course the Bills for the Loans, and for Public works I keep for the last, and until the House has done the other business which I want carried, as *they* are certain.

Your connexion with North American matters will terminate therefore most prosperously, and I think if anyone will compare the state of things two years ago when you sent me out to do *your* work, (and with no one but yourself could I have done it) with that which exists at present, no one will be found to affirm that any Secretary of State before ever produced half so great a change.

One Province without a Constitution, under arbitrary power—with scarcely any good laws—with its' whole frame work both of Society & administration completely disjointed—the other in a state of the greatest excitement and discontent—both without anything approaching to a Government or Departmental responsibility—Now, the constitution restored to one, and greatly improved for both—many most excellent institutions established by law in one, & improvements making (sic) in the other. The great and harassing questions of Church Reserves, & Responsible Govt settled—the Offices of Govt arranged so as to ensure responsibility in those who are at their head and an efficient discharge of their duties to the Governor and the Public. The Legislature assembled, acting in harmony with the Executive, and really employed in beneficial measures of Legislation. Public tranquility restored and the trade and immigration nearly doubled, I think that whoever may succeed you in the Colonial Department will hardly be able to present such a picture which I have not overcharged, and which I certainly do not paint in order to take credit to myself, for I repeat that it is to you that it is due, for no one could have been the immediate instrument of producing the change even if he had fifty times the talent or zeal which I can pretend to, if it had not been for *your* directions and encouragement, and for the assistance which *you* supplied in England.

I shall of course stay here till everything to be done this session is well through, and I have been enabled after its' close to do what is required in setting any new laws or institutions in operation—nothing therefore can now prevent or mar the most complete success and Canada

must henceforward go on well except it is most terribly
mismanaged.

What awful losses you have had in the Counties! I did
not think we had so many to lose. But your minority tho'
not so strong as I hoped, will still be enough to enforce
good measures or else to eject Peel hereafter, and perhaps
as it is not quite so large as was anticipated, it may be
more easily kept under control, & prevented from having
recourse to *violence*, the rock on which it is most likely
to split.

You will have received by the Halifax Steamer of the
4th a dispatch from Fox about McLeod; a very unsatis-
factory account of the state of things at Washington. Mr.
Webster by the bye informs him that the Hunter's Lodges
are again in full operation along the Frontier, and that
there is an intention of creating fresh disturbances and
even of committing fresh outrages on the people in
Canada—*he* thinks with the connivance and support of
a party *here*. I entirely disbelieve the last, but I have no
doubt of the first, and that the other is only a statement
made by the Refugees and the Border ruffians to delude
the people and get assistance for their schemes. I have
asked Fox to get Webster to send an officer to enquire,
but I have told him at the same time that if outrages are
really committed, and the State or General Authorities
will not interfere to prevent them, I will put them down
and punish the perpetrators without looking very nicely
to whether it be done by a violation of the United States
territory or not. If armed bands of Americans were to
assemble and actually cross to invade our territory,
because they were either suffered or could not be prevented
by their own Government, I am satisfied that we must

put an end to their proceedings ourselves let the consequences be what they may. But I confess I do not anticipate any such thing and I believe that it is talk as regards *invasion* and will remain so.

By the bye, if in the final clean up, you have any small commissionship or other office to be held by a Lawyer, I wish you would think of Dowling the Legal adviser whom you sent me out, & who will of course return with me. He is a most excellent person, and [The end of this letter is missing.].

GOVT. HOUSE KINGSTON 11th Augt. 1841

PRIVATE

MY DEAR LORD JOHN

I wrote to you so lately, (the 4th Augt. by the Gt. Western) that I have scarcely anything to trouble you with, and only write to say so—for altho' this may find you no longer in Downing St., you will not be the less interested I am sure in my proceedings.

The last week has been a good one for me, as 1 am now certain that my District Councils Bill for Upper Canada to which you know I attached so much importance as the complement to the Union Act, will pass, and that too, exactly as I framed the law for Lower Canada which I made so by ordinance. The certainty of a change of Ministry at home of course embarrasses me considerably by diminishing my power over opinion, & raising (however erroneously) the hopes of those who are adverse to my administration; but the combined efforts of the Ultra Tories, & Ultra Rads, the first of whom wish of course to stop a measure which gives so much popular power, whilst the latter desire to deprive it of all the checks against abuse, have signally failed.

I expect this Bill to be through by the end of the week, and then there will remain but little to prevent me from proroguing Parlt., for the other matters will go over easily and speedily enough.

The last accounts have brought me the conclusion of your Elections which are worse than I was led to expect, but after all it was impossible to look for much more, with such a host of interests arrayed against you, and only the "unprotected public" for you. Morpeth's defeat in the West Riding is the worst in *effect*, as it gives the Tories fair grounds for asserting that the Manufacturing Interests are at least divided upon your measure. The Yorkshire Clothiers and Flax Spinners deserve to be ruined for their folly! and they will stand a good chance of being so I am afraid, for it certainly would appear that between the difficulty of getting returns for goods caused by our exclusion of foreign articles, and the ruinous increase of manufacturing power abroad, their depression and distress in Trade in England is not likely to be relieved by leaving things alone—the Tory remedy. I am too much broken in health to take much more than the interest of a Spectator in the political struggle, if there be one, next session, and I shall not be at all sorry for the opportunity of trying by quiet and amusement to save the remains of my constitution; but I cannot but feel deeply anxious about the Country and I am very gloomy about its' prospects. The evil which ten years ago I predicted, if we did not liberalize our Commercial policy has fallen on it. We have successful rivals every where, and friends no where. Even the bold and gallant struggle you have made is misrepresented, and attributed not to its' true motives, or conviction of the truth of the principles of Free Trade, but to a desire to *mislead* other nations & prevent them from following you in your (*successful*!!) policy of protection and prohibition. That, however is no reason certainly for the folly and ingratitude of the English people for which they will pay dearly if I am not mistaken.

I have nothing fresh about American matters. The Whig Govt. has obtained so much power thro' the energy of Clay in the Senate that I should hope that the Executive will assume a little more responsibility and settle some matters. But it is very doubtful—the Presidential Contest for 1844 has begun again already, & the worst passions and prejudices of the mob will be consulted as much as before.

Believe me, ever
My dear Lord John
SYDENHAM

GOVT. HOUSE KINGSTON 28th Augt. 1841

PRIVATE

MY DEAR LORD JOHN

I have no letter from you, but you were too well & I trust too happily engaged when the last packet left for me to expect it.

Whether in or out of Downing St. you will I am sure be glad to learn that I have carried my great measure of the Districts Councils and yesterday went down to assent to it in the Queen's name. So that it is law now for the *whole Province*, and the Union Act has received the addition without which as I told you last year when you left out my clauses, it was in my opinion unmanageable. I have carried this Bill too exactly in the same terms as my ordinance for the Lower Province thereby setting up the Special Council Legislation by the sanction of the United Legislature. But every thing that I foretold in my despatch to you Sept last, when I was very nearly abandoning the concern for want of these clauses, came to pass. The Tories opposed the measure because it gave too much power to the People—the Radicals because it imposed checks on that power, and with *members* generally the Bill was most unpalatable, tho' they did not dare to avow the real motives of their dislike, because it is a death blow to their own jobbing for local purposes. The combination was so strong that on a most important clause in the Committee, that of the nomination of Wardens by the Crown, we could only throw out an amendment making them elective by the casting vote of the Chairman—the Tories actually voting for their election *by the People* in order to quash the Bill! After this shave however, everything went on prosperously and the measure passed by 42–30 in the Assembly, and unanimously in the Council without amendment. But there would not have been the slightest chance of getting such a law for the whole Province, if it had not already been enacted for Lower Canada.

Now it is impossible for any Governor or any Parliament to prevent the Union Act working well.

All my other measures are through too, except the Public works and the ways and means for such of them as may be decided on, but that is the affair of the Assembly exclusively and they may do what they like about it. I have given them a pretty good Bill of Fare to choose from,[167] which I send you in case you should not get the official dispatch. If not adopted now, it will be next session, which is as good, for the Country are wild for it.

The Parliament will therefore I hope be in a state to Prorogue in a fortnight or three weeks at furthest and then it will take me nearly as much longer to wind up, as I am determined to leave nothing unsettled which I can do. But at the end of that time, the middle of Octr. I trust that I shall hear the guns pealing from the Rock of Quebec and a most delightful sound it will be to me.

I am uneasy still about the Boundary and McLeod. The latter was to have been tried on the 19th, but was put off till today (the 28th) and I now fear that it is likely that the case will again be postponed. I do not see any way out of this mess.

I am impatient to know your first Parliamentary proceedings. Your address to Electors of London is admirable and I think must tell both with the Country and even the most violent of our supporters

Believe me, ever,

My dear Lord John

Yours most Truly

SYDENHAM

P.S. I have just learnt by a letter [from] Gardner & Bradly that McLeod's trial is put off to the Circuit which meets at Utica on the fourth Monday in September, and a Commission has issued from the Superior Court to Commission in Canada to collect evidence on the part of the "People" (the Persecutors) against McLeod.

ImpP & B. [?] Write to the Atty. Genl. to say that they will afford attendance on the part of McLeod at the nomination, for which I shall of course find funds as before, but I will not otherwise countenance or advise in the line of defence they may adopt for their Client.

GOVT. HOUSE KINGSTON 11*th Sept.* 1841[168]
PRIVATE

MY DEAR LORD JOHN

I have received you'rs of the 18th Augt. I am much obliged to you for the red ribbon[169] but a great deal more for the kind manner in which you recommended it.

You will have seen that I was determined to do all my business before coming away and a pretty session it will be; every measure will have been triumphantly carried and though I could not get the Bank through it must succeed another year. The House of Assembly wished to defer it for this session, but in the meantime they have taxed the issues of private Banks which will ensure its' passing;—my successor therefore will have little legislation even left for him.

I wish I could manage my own matters as well, but a week ago my horse fell with me, broke the great bone of my leg, and made a large hole above the knee; the accident is very painful especially as the gout, which cowardlike always takes one at a disadvantage has stepped in to add to my sufferings, and under any circumstances I fear that I must have three weeks or a month of bed. The doctors however tell me that I am sure to be in a state to be moved by water to Quebec in time to get off this autumn.

You will understand from this account of myself why
I write or rather dictate to you as little as possible.

Believe me my dear Lord John

Yours most Truly

SYDENHAM

This proved to be Lord Sydenham's last letter to Lord
John Russell. The following account of his death was
apparently written by Sydenham's secretary, Mr. T. W. C.
Murdoch, to his brother, Mr. G. Poulett Scrope.

KINGSTON 20 *Sept.* 1841[170]

[*Copy*]

MY DEAR SIR,

   I have written an Official Dispatch to Lord
Russel (sic) announcing Lord Sydenham's death because,
had I waited for Sir R. Jackson to do so the opportunity
of the Great Western would have been lost, and it would
not be right that the Secretary of State should learn this
most distressing but important event through the Newspapers only. To yourself and to Lord Sydenham's friends
it will be interesting to know particulars which it would
be impossible to put in an Official Despatch, and I
therefore add this private Letter.

  On the 4th Instant in riding home, Lord Sydenham's
horse fell and broke his leg inflicting at the same time
a deep and painful wound just above the knee. For about
a week he appeared to be going on tolerably well, though
of course his strength was affected by the confinement,
and although he repeatedly expressed doubts as to his
recovery there was nothing to lead us to suppose, nor did
the Medical men give us to understand that his present-

ment (sic) was more than the natural consequence of the lowness produced by weakness. On Monday however the 13th spasm came on first in the leg and afterwards in the stomach and throat; yet still we had no idea that a fatal result would ensue. The prorogation had at first been fixed for Wednesday, and afterwards at the request of the Assembly postponed till Friday. And so little prepared were we then for what was to follow, that during Thursday the Governor was employed in giving his decision on the several Bills which had been passed, and in revising the Draft of the Speech which at his desire I had prepared for him. On Friday Morning his illness increased so much that he was obliged to put off the prorogation—and as his illness was evidently advancing every hour, and his Medical men suggested that possibly delirium might ensue he determined to prorogue the Parliament by Deputation, General Clitherow being the Senior Military Officer present at Kingston was selected for the purpose and prorogued the Parliament on Saturday Morning at 12 o'clock, giving at the same time the Royal Assent or reservation to the Bills. In the latter of course he exercised no discretion, all the Bills having previously received Lord Sydenham's decision and almost all of them his Signature.

In the night of Friday occurred that great change which made it evident, that Lord Sydenham's illness was drawing rapidly to a fatal termination. Every one of his symptoms was fearfully aggravated; and even those who had before hoped most were forced to confess, that hope was vain. He was perfectly conscious of his own state and about 2 o'clock he and all his Establishment, received the Sacrament—he dictated to Mr. Dowling his Will,

making that Gentleman and Major Campbell, his Military
Secretary, his Executors in this province, he then took
leave of us all, desiring me as his last, Command "to write
the history of his Administration,"[171] He expressed
throughout, his continued interest in this Country, and
his satisfaction that the Parliament was prorogued. The
rest of that day and the whole night were spent by him
in prayer, and conversation with his Chaplain. He desired
to be remembered to Lord John Russel, saying of him,
when that part of his Will in which Lord John is mentioned was read to him "He was the noblest man, it ever
was my good fortune to know." To all his establishment,
he left some token of remembrance. During the whole of
Saturday and the following night, he suffered I fear very
much, but his mind never for an instant failed, nor
appeared to be clouded by his approaching death. Once
or twice his spasms were so severe, that we were afraid
he was gone, but it was not till 7 oclock on Sunday
morning, that we were summoned into his room, to see
him breathe his last. Since then the injury on his leg has
been examined, and has been found to be much more
severe than was supposed—so severe as to leave no
chance for a man whose health was so precarious as the
Governor's.

[T. W. C. MURDOCH]

Charles Poulett Thomson, first baron Sydenham, was
buried at Kingston, September 24, 1841.

NOTES

1. See memorandum of 1836 printed in *Select Documents on British Colonial Policy* 1830–1860. Edited by Kenneth N. Bell and W. P. Morrell (Oxford, 1928), 20–23.

2. See Russell to Melbourne, February 2, 1839. *Early Correspondence of Lord John Russell*. Edited by Rollo Russell (London, 1913), II, 244–245.

3. *Hansard*, third series, XLVIII, 965–966.

4. On the evening of June 28th, Peel again inquired about the government's intention regarding the bill in question. Lord John Russell replied that it would not be pressed forward to a second reading, and indicated that the government would follow the course suggested in this letter. *Hansard*, third series, XLVIII, 1007–1009.

5. The Marquis of Normanby had succeeded Lord Glenelg at the colonial office in February, 1839.

6. Among the Russell Papers is found the following Memorandum:
"At a Cabinet Meeting held at Lord Melbourne's on Wednesday the 21st of August 1839

Present

Melbourne, Lord Chancellor, Lord John Russell, Palmerston, Normanby, Minto, Spring Rice, Hobhouse, Duncannon, Holland, C. Poulett Thomson, and Lord Howick.

The Governor-General is authorized by the Cabinet to promise that Her Majesty's Government will submit to Parliament a proposal to guarantee a Loan to Upper Canada or to the United Province for the purpose of diminishing the Interest on the Debt and of continuing the Public Works, of a sum not exceeding £1,500,000 (One million and a half sterling).

This Loan is to be secured on the Revenues of the Upper Province, or of the United Province. This assistance is discretionary on the part of the Governor-General and only to be used in order to obtain the consent of the Provinces to what may be deemed by him a final and satisfactory settlement."

7. Viscount Howick, afterwards third Earl Grey and colonial secretary, 1846–52. At this time he was secretary at war in the Melbourne Ministry.

8. James Stephen, permanent under-secretary in and legal adviser for the colonial office.

9. Sir Francis Head, lieutenant-governor of Upper Canada, 1835–1837, had by direct appeals to the voters secured a conservative majority in the legislative assembly of the province.

10. Spencer Walpole, *The Life of Lord John Russell* (London, 1891), I, 349; G. Poulett Scrope, *Memoir of the Life of the Right Honourable Charles Lord Sydenham* (London, 1843), 100.

11. *Early Correspondence of Lord John Russell*, II, 256.

12. On August 27th new writ was moved for his constituency, Manchester, and two days later he was sworn into his new office. Scrope, *Life of Sydenham*, 100.

13. Lord John Russell and Lord Normanby exchanged offices at this time. Normanby took the home office and Russell the colonial office. In a minute on salaries, sent to the lords of the treasury September 2nd, Russell recommended that Thomson should be granted a salary of £7000 and allowed £3000 for outfit. Expenses connected with moving from Lower to Upper Canada, securing houses, etc., should be borne by the public. The treasury agreed (Pennington to Stephen, September 6th) and Thomson was informed of this September 8th. The Public Archives of Canada, G. Series, vol. 43, pp. 133–145.

14. See Note 6.

15. For extracts from this article see Adam Shortt, *Lord Sydenham*, (Toronto, 1908), 141.

16. Edward Ellice, from his early connections with the fur trade of the American Northwest known as "the Bear" or "Bear Ellice."

17. This had been suggested in the *Colonial Gazette*.

18. Lieutenant-governor of Upper Canada.

19. The Maine–New Brunswick boundary controversy.

20. Lieutenant-governor of New Brunswick.

21. Thomson's ship cast anchor at Quebec October 17th, but he awaited the arrival of the acting governor-general, Sir John Colborne (later Lord Seaton) from Montreal, and did not land till October 19th. Thomson to Russell, October 19th, 1839. Canadian Archives, Q Series, vol. 261, p. 43.

22. Russell Ellice in a letter to Lord Melbourne dated August 22, 1839, protested in behalf of the Committee of the North American Colonial Association against the appointment of C. Poulett Thomson as governor-general of Canada. Melbourne replied drily, August 24th, that the sentiments of the Association could not have been better expressed. For text of these letters see *The Times*, August 31, 1839. See also Scrope, *Life of Sydenham*, 105, and Shortt, *Sydenham*, 132.

23. "I have much satisfaction in reporting these proofs that the efforts made in some quarters to prejudice the minds of the people of Canada, against the selection which Her Majesty was graciously pleased to make of Governor of British North America, have been unsuccessful, at least in Quebec." Thomson to Russell, October 22, 1839. Canadian Archives, Q. Series, vol. 261, p. 77.

24. See note 22.

25. Sir John Colborne, afterwards Lord Seaton, commander-in-chief and governor-general of Canada in the interim between the departure of Lord Durham and the arrival of Thomson.

26. Sir George Arthur, lieutenant-governor of Upper Canada.

27. James Stuart, chief justice of the Court of Queen's Bench, Montreal, and president of the Special Council of Lower Canada.

28. The Union Bill.

29. For account of journey see Scrope, *Life of Sydenham*, 141, note.

30. Thomson to Russell, November 18, 1839. Canadian Archives, Q. Series, vol. 261, pp. 176–181.

31. C. A. Hagerman. A discussion of the attitude of Messrs. Hagerman and Draper on the Union Bill is found in Thomson to Russell, December 23, 1839, "Confidential." Canadian Archives, Q. Series, vol. 262, pp. 121–123.

32. W. H. Draper.

33. For a similar account of his impressions see extracts of letters of November 20th and December 8th, Scrope, *Life of Sydenham*, 148–151.

34. John Beverly Robinson, a leader of the Family Compact, was in England on account of his health and used the opportunity to work against the Canadian program of the government. It required questions in the House of Commons and rather stern orders from Lord John Russell to get him to return to his post. Canadian Archives, G. Series, vol. 46, pp. 93, 565–595.

35. A full account of the vote in the Legislative Council is found in Thomson to Russell, December 14, 1839, No. 21. Canadian Archives, Q. Series, vol. 262, pp. 83–85. See also Scrope, *Life of Sydenham*, 142–143.

36. Dr. John Strachan, Anglican bishop of Toronto.

37. Sir John Colborne had left Quebec October 23rd on the *Pique*, landed at Plymouth November 17th, and before the end of the month he was made Baron Seaton for his services in Canada.

38. Vote is given as 28 to 20 in Thomson to Russell, January 22, 1840.

39. Extracts from this letter are printed in Scrope, *Life of Sydenham*, 168–169.

40. Vote is given as 13 to 5 in dispatch to Russell of January 22, 1840. Scrope gives an extract from this letter, *Life of Sydenham*, 169.

41. Petition was dated January 15, 1840, and enclosed with Thomson to Sydenham February 5, 1840, No. 90. Canadian Archives, Q. Series, vol. 270, part 2, pp. 351–353. The petition was the work of Bishop Strachan.

42. Henry Philpotts, bishop of Exeter, later led the fight in the House of Lords against Thomson's plan for settling the Clergy Reserves question.

43. Presented to Parliament March 23, 1840.

44. Enclosure with Thomson to Russell January 22, 1840, "Confidential." Canadian Archives, Q.Series, vol. 270, part 1, pp. 140–235.

45. J. W. Pringle came out with Thomson in 1839 to arrange "for the Representation, on the principles of the Union Bill, and for the formation of Municipal Districts, etc.—also to report to him, as an Engineer, on the Public Works of the Province." He was gazetted as civil secretary for Lower Canada with no salary. The imperial government ultimately rewarded him for his services in Canada. See Canadian Archives, G. Series, vol. 51, pp. 466–473, and Duplicate Despatches, 1841, vol. 54, pp. 386–388.

46. Scrope gives some sentences from this letter. *Life of Sydenham*, 171–172.

47. The legislature of Upper Canada was prorogued February 10, 1840. For the speech see Canadian Archives, Q. Series, vol. 270, part 2, pp. 462–464.

48. For the text of this dispatch see W. P. M. Kennedy, *Documents of the Canadian Constitution 1759–1915* (Toronto, 1918), 522–524.

49. Robert Baldwin, the leader of the reform party, was made solicitor general of Upper Canada in February 1840. Subsequent events showed that he had not abandoned his views on responsible government.

50. Russell to Thomson, December 16, 1839. No. 53. Canadian Archives, Q. Series, vol. 270, part 2, pp. 515–517.

51. Question was also argued at considerable length in dispatch of this date, February 13, 1840. *Ibid.*, 510–514.

52. No. 44. February 12, 1840. *Ibid.*, 465–470. For an account of this controversy see Egerton Ryerson, *The Story of My Life* (Toronto, 1883), 269–290.

53. James Stephen, the permanent under-secretary of state for the colonies.

54. For an account of Aler's visit to Canada see Ryerson, *Story of My Life*, 242–243.

55. Ryerson defended Thomson's plan in regard to the Clergy Reserves against Bishop Strachan, and in general supported Thomson's policy and measures in the *Guardian*. *Ibid.*, 262–265.

56. Thomson to Russell, February 13, 1840. "Confidential." Canadian Archives, Q. Series, vol. 270, part 3, pp. 528–535.

57. Thomson doubtless had in mind the disappointing results of the Canadian Revenue Control Act, 1831 (1 & 2, William IV, c. 23). For discussion of this act see W. P. M. Kennedy, *The Constitution of Canada* (London, 1922), 106 ff.

58. Speech from the Throne. Lord Durham believed that Thomson had succeeded and wrote to Russell, March 26, 1840, "I sincerely

rejoice in Thomson's success. He will have already told you that I contributed to it to the utmost of my ability." Walpole, *Life of Russell*, I, 397.

59. Scrope, *Life of Sydenham*, 173.

60. The bishop of Exeter. His name is sometimes spelled "Phillpotts" and other times "Philpotts."

61. Bishop Strachan.

62. Parts of this paragraph are found in Scrope, *Life of Sydenham*, 175–176. However, he gives additional material apparently taken from another letter.

63. Sir John Harvey, lieutenant-governor of New Brunswick.

64. Sir Richard Jackson, the commander-in-chief. This paragraph deals, of course, with the Maine–New Brunswick boundary dispute.

65. John Neilson, editor of the *Quebec Gazette*, had sponsored a petition against the union of the two provinces.

66. Thomson to Russell, May 22, 1840, "Private and Confidential," discussed at considerable length the advantages and otherwise of Bytown (Ottawa), Quebec, Montreal, Toronto, and Kingston. He favored the last as capital of united Canada, and Russell agreed with him (June 22, 1840). Canadian Archives, Q. Series, vol. 272, part 1, pp. 144–160.

67. The Toronto *Examiner*, edited by Francis Hincks.

68. Edited by Egerton Ryerson.

69. Chancellor of the exchequer in the existing Melbourne government. Thomson had been considered for this post when Spring Rice resigned in August 1839.

70. In dispatch marked "Separate" of March 12, 1840, Thomson complained of the inconveniences resulting from the failure to put private letters in the official bag and entrust them all to a messenger. Russel replied, April 17th, that the request had been granted. Canadian Archives, Q. Series, vol. 271, part 1, pp. 46–50.

71. Sir Colin Campbell, lieutenant-governor of Nova Scotia, was engaged in a bitter conflict with the reform party of the province led by Joseph Howe.

72. Viscount Duncannon, later 4th earl of Bessborough, lord privy seal in the Melbourne government.

73. This letter was apparently addressed to Lord Duncannon.

74.   DOWNING STREET, 20*th March*, 1840
SIR,

"Her Majesty has directed me to express to you Her Gracious approbation of the various steps which you have taken in order to procure the adjustment of the differences which have so long prevailed in Canada.

The promptitude with which you have acted in ascertaining the sentiments of the Special Council;—the decision which you made to resort in person to the Upper Province;—the conciliatory spirit in which you met the Legislature of that Province;—and the zeal for Her Majesty's Service, and the good of Her People, which you have, on all occasions evinced, have been observed by the Queen with the greatest satisfaction, and have inspired Her Majesty with a confident hope that you may successfully complete the Work you have so ably commenced."

Russell to Thomson, No. 90. Canadian Archives, G. Series, vol. 46, pp. 553–555.

75. *Hansard*, third series, LII, 1323–1342.

76. Question discussed in Thomson to Russell, April 25, 1840, "Confidential." Russell replied, June 5, 1840, that in consequence of Thomson's representations the 15th and 17th clauses had been changed, giving two members to the county of Lincoln. Canadian Archives, Q. Series, vol. 271, part 2, pp. 385–387.

77. Thomson to Russell, May 5, 1840, No. 102. *Ibid.*, vol. 272, part 1, pp. 73–77.

78. Mr. J. S. Pakington asked questions regarding Bishop Strachan's salary in the House of Commons March 30, 1840. *Hansard*, third series, LIII, 231. The dispatch referred to is No. 99 of May 2, 1840, which contained numerous enclosures. Thomson claimed that Dr. Strachan had for several years drawn an annual salary of £250 as president of King's College, though the institution had not been established. Canadian Archives, Q. Series, vol. 272, part 1, pp. 20–45. See also *Canada and Its Provinces*, Edited by Adam Shortt and Arthur G. Doughty (Toronto, 1914–1917), V, 21–22.

79. For detailed analysis see Thomson to Russell, May 6, 1840, "Confidential." Canadian Archives, Q. Series, vol. 272, part 1, pp. 86–96.

80. Chief Justice Stuart.

81. *Hansard*, third series, LIII, 661–662.

82. Mr. Edward Dowling was sent out in this capacity. Russell to Thomson, June 30, 1840, "Separate." See also Sydenham to Russell October 19, 1840, No. 182. Canadian Archives, Q. Series, vol. 273, part 3, pp. 490–493.

83. In regard to Thomson's peerage, Russell wrote to Melbourne, April 26, 1840: "I think your taking the Queen's pleasure fully discharges your engagement to Thomson—On his side he has done all that it was possible for him to do to bring the Canadian affairs to a termination, and his having done it in five months instead of ten is only so much the more to his credit—The rest remains for us, and he ought not to suffer, if we bungle, or Lyndhurst is factious." Russell Papers, Public Record Office.

84. Chief Justice Stuart was made a baronet in 1840.

85. The question was brought before the House of Commons, May 28, 1840. *Hansard*, third series, LIV, 701.

86. Lord Ripon, formerly Lord Goderich.

87. Thomson gave his views on the situation in Nova Scotia at considerable length in dispatch marked "Confidential," May 27, 1840. Canadian Archives, Q. Series, vol. 272, part 1, pp. 214–220.

88. Henry S. Fox, British minister to Washington.

89. For an extract from this letter see Scrope, *Life of Sydenham*, 181.

90. J. R. Ogden.

91. For survey of legislative work see Thomson to Russell, June 27, 1840, No. 128. Canadian Archives, Q. Series, vol. 272, part 2, pp. 256–360.

92. Edward Ellice. Sydenham and Ellice were reconciled before the death of the former. Writing to Lord John Russell, October 28, 1841, Ellice paid a strong tribute to Sydenham, and added: "I believe you knew—a most consolatory reflexion to me—that we were again in habits of confidential correspondence." Original MS. the Russell Papers.

93. *Hansard*, third series, LIV, 813.

94. *Ibid.*, 701–707.

95. *Ibid.*, LIII, 644–646.

96. For an account of the affair at Shorthills, June 1838, see William Kingsford, *The History of Canada* (1887–1898), X, 479–481.

97. Thomson to Russell, June 27, 1840, "Confidential." Canadian Archives, Q. Series, vol. 272, part 2, pp. 462–468.

98. In the debate on Lord Stanley's bill for Registration of Voters (Ireland), May 19, 1840, C. Wood and Lord Howick opposed Lord John Russell. *Hansard*, third series, LIV, 352–358, 367–374.

99. In printing portions from this letter, Scrope has, of course, deleted the comments on Sir Colin Campbell, and also made some verbal changes. See *Life of Sydenham*, 185–189.

100. See *The Speeches and Public Letters of Joseph Howe*, ed. by J. A. Chisholm (Halifax, 1909), I, 327–328; W. Ross Livingston, *Responsible Government in Nova Scotia* (Iowa City, 1930), 130–131; Chester Martin, *Empire and Commonwealth* (Oxford, 1929), 195–198.

101. Marked "Confidential," July 27, 1840. Canadian Archives, Q. Series, vol. 273, part 1, pp. 83–106. See also Scrope, *Life of Sydenham*, 183–185.

102. Herbert Huntington, friend and ally of Joseph Howe.

103. William, later Sir William, Young was one of Howe's supporters.

104. Sir Colin Campbell was made governor of Ceylon upon his removal from Nova Scotia, in September 1840.

105. Duke of Wellington. The reference is doubtless to the duke's

formal protest against the third reading of the Act of Union, House of Lords, July 13, 1840. *Hansard*, third series, LV, 662–666.

106. Scrope, *Life of Sydenham*, 190–194.

107. For detailed criticism of the Act of Union see dispatch No. 160, Toronto, September 16, 1840. Canadian Archives, Q. Series, vol. 273, part 2, pp. 276–293.

108. Apparently reference is to Edward Ellice.

109. Major-general John Clitherow.

110. Major-General Sir James Macdonnell.

111. Later Lord Taunton, president of the board of trade.

112. T. B., later Lord, Macaulay, had succeeded Lord Howick as secretary at war.

113. Lord privy seal and member of the cabinet.

114. Lord Falkland, newly-appointed lieutenant-governor of Nova Scotia.

115. See *British.Parliamentary Papers*, August 8, 1840.

116. For further discussion see Sydenham to Russell, October 9, 1840, No. 176, and Russell to Sydenham, February 17, 1840, No. 308 with enclosures. Canadian Archives, Q. Series, vol. 273, part 3, pp. 428–431, 437.

117. R. B. Sullivan, president of the executive council of Upper Canada, was also commissioner of crown lands. His numerous public duties prevented him from supervising his subordinates, two of whom, in the office of crown lands, had misappropriated public funds. The money was restored by Sullivan, and he was later re-imbursed in the form of salary for some of his non-salaried offices. See Sydenham to Russell, October 12, 1840, No. 178, and Russell's reply, *Ibid.*, pp. 447–452.

118. French minister of marine and the colonies.

119. For further discussion of this bill see letter of November 23, 1840. Scrope, *Life of Sydenham*, 207.

120. The boundary dispute was discussed in another letter of this date. *Ibid.*, 313–314.

121. The later Empress Frederick of Germany, born November 21, 1840.

122. The Act of Union referred to "the Governor-General of the two Provinces of Upper and Lower Canada," but Sydenham's commission did not contain this designation, and doubts had arisen whether a new commission might not be necessary. These were set to rest by Russell to Sydenham, November 12, 1840, No. 258. Canadian Archives, G. Series, vol. 50, pp. 37–42.

123. Robert R. Gillespie, London representative and partner in the firm Gillespie, Moffatt, Finlay & Co.

124. Nevertheless Sydenham included George Moffatt in the list of prospective members of the Legislative Council for Canada. See

Sydenham to Russell, February 23, 1841. Canadian Archives Duplicate Despatches, 1841, vol. 54, pp. 281–289. See also private letter of Sydenham to Moffatt of March 11, 1841, in *Portraits of British Americans*, by W. Notman (Montreal, 1865), I, 113.

125. For private relations between General Winfield Scott of the U.S. army, and Sir John Harvey see Marcus T. Wright, *General Scott* (New York, 1894), 143–144.

126. Governor of Maine.

127. Boundary question discussed in Sydenham to Russell November 23, No. 196, and December 28, 1840, "Confidential." Canadian Archives, Q. Series, vol. 274, part 1, pp. 36–67, and *Ibid.*, part 2, pp. 328–332. See also letter of December 26, 1840, Scrope, *Life of Sydenham*, pp. 314–315. Partly, no doubt, as a result of the strong representations made by Lord Sydenham, Sir John Harvey was recalled. In commenting upon Russell's dispatch to Harvey asking him to come home, Lord Palmerston said: "His [i.e. Harvey's] Folly and weakness and his Perseverance in meddling with matters which he has no authority to deal with, and which he has repeatedly during the last two years been ordered to abstain from, have done us great mischief." Palmerston to Russell, January 19, 1841, Original MS., the Russell Papers.

128. General William Henry Harrison elected president of the United States, November 1840.

129. Reference is apparently to the fourth annual message of President Van Buren, December 5, 1840. See James D. Richardson, *A Compilation of the Messages and Papers of the Presidents*, 1789–1897 (Washington, 1896), III, 603–604.

130. James McNab of Nova Scotia.

131. Sydenham's opinions on the prospects for the election and an account of some of the preparations made by him are found in dispatch marked "Confidential," February 26, 1841. Canadian Archives, Duplicate Dispatches, vol. 54, pp. 303–313.

132. Dispatch of February 23, 1841, "Confidential." *Ibid.*, 281–289.

133. Alexander McLeod had been a member of the party led by Captain Andrew Drew that crossed to the American side and there seized and destroyed the "Caroline," December 29, 1837, because the ship had been used by rebels in making raids on Canada. McLeod was later arrested in the state of New York and tried for murder. For a brief account of this celebrated affair see Hugh L. Keenleyside, *Canada and the United States* (New York, 1929), pp. 113–114. Sydenham had discussed it in a letter to Lord John Russell, of January 28, 1840. Scrope, *Life of Sydenham*, pp. 235–237.

134. Nickname given to President Harrison. He died a month after his inauguration, April 4, 1841.

135. *Hansard*, third series, LVII, 194–214.

136. The Bishop of Exeter urged that the Queen's assent should be withheld from an ordinance passed by the Special Council of Lower Canada incorporating the Seminary of St. Sulpice in Montreal.

137. For Sir Alured Clarke, see *Documents Relating to the Constitutional History of Canada*, ed. by Arthur G. Doughty and Duncan A. McArthur (Ottawa, 1914), p. 54 and note 2.

138. This question was further discussed in confidential dispatches of April 9 and 12, 1840. Canadian Archives, Duplicate Dispatches, 1841, vol. 54, pp. 442–449.

139. See W. P. Morrell, *British Colonial Policy in the Age of Peel and Russell* (Oxford, 1930), 171–173.

140. The reference is apparently to a report on the burning of the "Caroline" and the McLeod affair by F. W. Pickens, chairman of the committee on foreign relations, February 18, 1841. See *State Documents*, 26th Congress, 2d Session, No. 162.

141. See also Scrope, *Life of Sydenham*, 318–319.

142. See *Hansard*, third series, LVII, 214–242, and letter of April 18, 1840, in Scrope, *Life of Sydenham*, 321–322.

143. Memorial from the British American Land Company, the Canada Company, and the North American Colonial Association of Ireland accompanied Russell's dispatch of March 26, No. 344. Canadian Archives, G. Series, vol. 108, pp. 419–446.

144. As agent for the companies.

145. The law officers in England retracted their former opinion and the naturalization ordinances were restored. See Sydenham to Russell, April 26, 1841, No. 53. Canadian Archives, Duplicate Dispatches, 1841, vol. 54, pp. 473–475, and Russell to Sydenham, June 30, 1841, No. 392; *ibid.*, G. Series, vol. 110. p. 59.

146. Sir William Colebrooke, who succeeded Harvey as Lieutenant-governor of New Brunswick.

147. See Russell to Sydenham, May 3, 1841, No. 369. Canadian Archives, G. Series, vol. 109, pp. 360–380. This dispatch reached Sydenham, May 22nd.

148. Captain Andrew Drew who had led in the attack on the "Caroline."

149. Lord John Russell gave notice, April 30, 1841, that on May 31st he would move "that the House resolves itself into a committee of the whole" to consider the Corn Laws. *Hansard*, third series, LVII, 1294.

150. Reference is to the budget prepared by the Melbourne ministry. See *ibid.*, 1295–1318.

151. The North American Colonial Association of Ireland had acquired the seigniory of Beauharnois in Lower Canada. Sydenham later changed his opinion of Wakefield and the company which he

represented. See Sydenham to Russell, July 26, 1841, No. 97. Canadian Archives, G. Series, vol. 454, pp. 133–135.

152. Point explained in Sydenham to Russell, May 25, 1841, No. 64. *Ibid.*, Duplicate Dispatches, Canada, 1841, vol. 54, pp. 516–522. See also J. L. Morison, *British Supremacy and Canadian Self-Government* (Glasgow, 1919), 112–113.

153. No. 369, *op. cit.*

154. This paragraph is printed in Scrope, *Life of Sydenham*, 234.

155. See Martin, *Empire and Commonwealth*, 256–262.

156. S. B. Harrison, provincial secretary of Canada, 1841–1843.

157. In the House of Commons, May 27, 1841. Sydenham had seen the report in *The Times*. For Peel's remarks see *Hansard*, third series, LVIII. 823–824.

The dispatch alluded to is No. 78 of June 23, 1841. Canadian Archives, Duplicate Dispatches, Canada, 1841, vol. 54, pp. 585–588.

158. June 26, 1841, "Confidential." *Ibid.*, pp. 612–633.

159. Senior officer "on the Lakes in Canada." Complaint against him stated by Sydenham to Russell, July 1, 1841, No. 86. Canadian Archives, G. Series, vol. 454, pp. 102–103.

160. Another letter of the same date is printed by Scrope, *Life of Sydenham*, 244–245.

161. Some of this ground is traversed with greater care in a letter of July 11, 1841. Scrope, *Life of Sydenham*, 248–249.

162. Scrope prints an extract from this letter with some verbal changes. *Life of Sydenham*, p. 250.

163. Decision of supreme court of New York not to release McLeod on a writ of *Habeas Corpus*.

164. The queen decided to confer the G.C.B. upon Sydenham when she accepted his resignation. Russell to Sydenham, August 18, 1841. Canadian Archives, Duplicate Dispatches, Canada, 1841, vol. 54, p. 639.

165. For extract, with some alterations, see Scrope, *Life of Sydenham*, 251–252.

166. No. 100, August 4, 1841. Canadian Archives, G. Series, vol. 454, pp. 139–141.

167. Greater portion of this letter printed in Scrope, *Life of Sydenham*, 252–253.

168. *Ibid.*, 261.

169. The G.C.B., see *ante* note, 164.

170. From copy found among the Russell Papers.

171. See Scrope, *Life of Sydenham*, V.

INDEX